NAVIGATION SKILLS FOR WALKERS

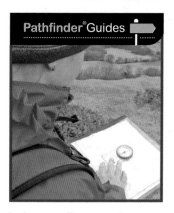

Map Reading,
Compass and GPS

Terry Marsh

Published by Milestone Publishing Limited under licence from Ordnance Survey Limited.
Pathfinder, Ordnance Survey, OS and the OS logos are registered trademarks of Ordnance Survey Limited and are used under licence from Ordnance Survey Limited.

Text © Terry Marsh, 2022
The moral right of the author has been asserted.

This product includes mapping data licensed from Ordnance Survey
© Crown copyright and databases rights (2022) OS 150002047

Photography:	Terry Marsh
	Front cover image: © Kuznetov_Konstantin/Shutterstock
	Images of GPS devices courtesy of Garmin (Europe) Ltd.,
	Satmap and Ordnance Survey.
Design:	Ark Creative (UK) Ltd.

ISBN 978-0-31909-175-3

This guide incorporates updated and rewritten content from Pathfinder® Guide Map Reading Skills (ISBN 978-0-7117-4978-8) and Pathfinder® Guide GPS for Walkers (ISBN 978-0-7117-4445-5), both by the publisher but now superseded and out of print.

First published in 2019 by Crimson Publishing.

First published 2021 by Trotman Publishing.

This edition first published 2022 by Milestone Publishing.

Milestone Publishing, 19-21D Charles Street, Bath, BA1 1HX
www.pathfinderwalks.co.uk

Printed in India by Replika Press Pvt. Ltd. 3/22

A catalogue record of this book is available from the British Library.

Contents

Foreword

Proven navigation skills will significantly enhance wayfinding and greatly improve walking safety and enjoyment. The pages that follow use illustrated and easy-to-follow guidelines to develop a toolkit for walkers in complementary navigation skills: map reading, map and compass, and GPS.

Here you will find an introduction to Ordnance Survey's Landranger and Explorer mapping, and to OS Maps, the Ordnance Survey's digital portal to leisure mapping for the whole of Britain at different scales, with its enormous benefits for planning, following and sharing walks.

Step-by-step guidance is given to understanding maps and building confidence and competence in how to read them. Route finding using map and compass and learning how to make the most of your GPS device equips the reader with practical techniques for successful navigation and for acquiring potentially life-saving skills.

Having these skills has gifted the author an unbridled enthusiasm and exuberant delight in the British and European countryside for almost 50 years, especially walking in mountain regions, and to do so with confidence and in safety. In this guide, he passes on the fruits of his experience.

Terry Marsh, May 2019

Map reading

Reading maps is easy; you simply unfold them, put them the right way up, find what you're looking for on the map, and then plot your route or your location.

Except, of course, it isn't quite that simple. Some fortunate people can look at a map, understand what it's all about, and take to it instantly. The majority are not so blessed, and understanding and getting the most out of maps takes a little more effort. I was one of the lucky ones, but didn't realise it until, during the first of many years teaching about map reading and basic navigation at a local adult education centre, I suddenly realised that I didn't know how to explain the things I was doing instinctively. This induced panic, which gradually transformed into methodology and then a comprehensive set of notes that now form the foundation of this book.

But there really is no mystery to reading maps; it is all very logical because everything on a map means something.

And now is an excellent time to begin map reading because Ordnance Survey's maps for walkers show newly agreed areas of Coastal Access, as well as Access Land, where you can explore freely; they use the latest technology in map production, and they are as up-to-date as can be. It's just a question of sitting down – and also getting out into the countryside – then working your way through the lines and dots and symbols stage by stage. That all these wonderful maps are now also available in digital format in the form of *OS Maps* is just an added bonus.

It is frustrating to enjoy walking in the countryside but to lack the confidence to read maps sufficiently well to be able to plot new routes or explore beyond the limits of walking guidebooks. This book will help you along the way, literally.

The trouble with maps

The first thing to realise about maps is that unlike the three-dimensional world in which we live, maps are printed on flat sheets of paper, and are therefore two-dimensional. This means that cartographers, those remarkably clever people who make maps, have to devise a means of showing three-dimensional information in a two-dimensional format. And in a way that is at least moderately intelligible.

The second oddity about maps is that while they are remarkably accurate, from another point of view they are incredibly inaccurate. This is partly because to make them manageable they have to be designed to a scale that crams a value-for-money amount of information onto a folded sheet of paper that doesn't require an estate car to carry it around. Something has to give; when you squeeze 20 kilometres' worth of information into less than one metre, it simply isn't possible to show every detail.

The way map-makers deal with this 'compression', getting a lot into a little, is by using a technique called 'scale'. Scale can be very confusing, but only if you think about it too much.

Understanding scale

Let's look at an illustration: I want to do a plan of my housing estate. It isn't a very big estate, probably just 100 metres in each direction. Now, I could get a sheet of drawing film that is also 100 metres in each direction, and measure everything very, very accurately, and plot it all on my huge piece of paper. But then there isn't room in my house for such a massive plan, and there is a limit to how many times I can fold it – eight apparently.

No, what I want to do is put everything onto a piece of paper measuring just one metre in each direction. So, what I have to come up with is a system that allows me to take one unit of measurement of the actual estate, and substitute a much smaller unit of measurement to represent the larger unit. It doesn't matter what units I choose; I just have to be smart enough to come up with something that fits my one-metre square sheet of paper.

What I could do, for example, is to take one metre of the 'real' world, and show it on my piece of paper as one centimetre. One metre equals one centimetre; so 100 metres (the size of my estate) equals 100 centimetres, which fits neatly onto my piece of paper, which is 100 centimetres wide. What I've done is to use scale in order to make things fit.

That's all scale is. Making things fit.

So what scale is best for walking?

A map drawn to a large scale, i.e. my 'one metre equals one centimetre' map, shows a lot of information. At the other extreme, a map on which one kilometre is represented by one centimetre, crams more 'distance' into the map, but contains much less detailed information. The latter would be good for motoring, the former, i.e. large-scale, is good for walking. A large-scale map will show rivers and streams fairly accurately along with field boundaries and individual buildings as well as other detailed features.

For many years the walker's 'map bible' was the Ordnance Survey *One-Inch* map (first created in 1801 for the area of Kent), on which one inch represented one statute mile. The scale, for the mathematically minded, was 1:63360, i.e. one unit of measurement (be it an inch or a foot, or whatever) on the map equated with 63,360 units of the same measurement on the ground. These early maps were a revelation, and much-prized by walkers. Even today, some of them are collectors' items. It took 190 maps to cover the whole of Britain.

When conversion to metric began, an adjustment to the scale was introduced. So, it became 1:50000, or 1¼ inches to 1 mile. With slightly more space on the map given to the same area as the older maps, these new maps were an improvement, but were simply an enlarged version of the *One-Inch* maps. Eventually, we were treated to new maps re-surveyed at the larger 1:50000 scale; these became what today are known as the *Landranger* maps. To cover the whole of Britain 204 maps are needed.

The reasons why these changes occurred are not vital; suffice to say, things became even better when maps appeared to a scale of 1:25000, or 2½ inches to 1 mile. Today, Ordnance Survey maps at this scale are part of the *Explorer* series. A total of 403 maps are in the 1:25000 series. Map extracts at the different scales are depicted in Figure 1, p11.

Unlike the *One-Inch* and *Landranger* maps, when the *Explorer* map series was completed, a number of 'combined' or 'special' maps were produced that did not fit into the format of the standard maps, but which were specifically intended to meet the needs of visitors to popular destinations like the Lake District, the Yorkshire Dales, and so on. These special maps were called *Outdoor Leisure* maps, but they are essentially *Explorer* maps joined together to deal with particular areas.

If there is a problem with the Ordnance Survey *Explorer* and *Outdoor Leisure* maps it is simply that they are intended to serve a number of purposes, and are not exclusively for walkers. So, information appears on the maps, such as the location of craft centres, fishing areas, country parks and caravan sites, which is not vital to walking.

When you are familiar with maps at all scales, it becomes readily obvious that those at 1:25000 are by far the best for walking, and these are the maps ordinarily used in *Pathfinder® Guides* (although occasionally slightly reduced in order to fit the pages).

Are there any problems with maps?

Well, yes, there are.

To begin with maps cannot be wholly accurate. In fact, it's safe to say that a map is in some way out-of-date the moment it is published. Changes are happening all the time and it is inordinately complex to keep track of them. Ordnance Survey has a mapping intelligence unit responsible for keeping track of all changes, and then feeding them through to the master maps. Even so, there are instances where, for example, field boundaries physically removed 40 years ago, still appear on maps. There is scope for improvement, as in all things, but realistically a modern Ordnance Survey map is as good as it gets.

Fig. 1: Maps of Skiddaw in the Lake District at different scales

One-inch map

1:50000 map

1:25000 map

Understanding 'North'

Some people have the uncanny knack of being able to spin round and face north; most of us just spin. In fact, it isn't a knack at all, it's a semi-conscious assimilation of basic information we are all aware of – the sun rises in the east and sets in the west and is roughly south at midday. If it's lunchtime, and you have your back to the sun (or where the sun would be if you could see it), then you are roughly facing north. Of course, we have the changes to accommodate 'summer time' to contend with. But as a rough guide, this system works... roughly.

This may seem like trivial information, but awareness, even at a subliminal level, of where the sun is, and where it should be (approximately) in relation to your intended direction-of-travel, will often strike a note of confidence in your mind... or ring alarm bells! It's all part of the art of navigation.

So, where is north?

Without maps or compasses there would be only one 'North', that we commonly call the North Pole. When not otherwise qualified, the term **North Pole** usually refers to the **Geographic North Pole** – the northernmost point on the surface of the Earth, where the axis on which it spins intersects the Earth's surface. It's way up there in the middle of the frozen Arctic Ocean. For mapping purposes, this is called **True North**, and for walking needs, it can be disregarded – unless you're walking to the North Pole.

To make life difficult, there are a number of other 'Norths', two of which are important to map reading and navigation:

- **North Magnetic Pole** – the Earth's magnetic field has two magnetic poles, one (currently) in the Arctic Ocean, referred to as the North Magnetic Pole (see Figure 2), and one off the coast of Antarctica, south of Australia, referred to as the South Magnetic Pole. At the North Magnetic Pole, the Earth's magnetic field is directed vertically downward relative to the Earth's surface. North Magnetic Pole is the eventual destination for a walker who follows the compass needle from anywhere on Earth. Unfortunately, the North Magnetic Pole is constantly moving due to the spinning of molten iron and nickel nearly 2,000 miles below the surface of the Earth. This can be as much as 60km per year, currently (2019) heading towards Russia. For the purposes of this book, the position of the North Magnetic Pole is called Magnetic

North. Put simply, it's where your compass needle points.

- **Grid North** – this is the direction of those vertical pale blue lines that, with those running east–west, form a grid on maps. Put simply, it's the top of the map.

> Magnetic North is where your compass needle points.

Fig. 2: The position of the North Magnetic Pole in 2017

Information about the relationship between true, grid and magnetic north is printed in the marginal data of maps as shown in Figure 3.

If you compare the section on North Points in the marginal data of maps, you'll find that there are variations from map to map. This is not because the True North has changed but rather that the map represents a different part of the country, and so the angle to True North is different.

The horizontal angular difference between Grid North and Magnetic North is called **grid magnetic angle** or **magnetic variation**. This angle is particularly important when you come to using map and compass, and will be returned to in the chapter on 'Using compasses'.

> Grid North is the top of the map.

Fig. 3: True, Grid and Magnetic North (extract from Explorer 296)

NORTH POINTS

At the centre of this sheet true north is 0°44' east of grid north.

Magnetic north is estimated at 0°30' west of grid north for July 2020.

Annual change is approximately 12' east.

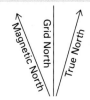

Grid lines and grid references

Brief mention was made in the last chapter of that network of thin pale blue lines superimposed on maps. This is called the **National Grid**. The National Grid is a unique reference system that can be applied to the British Isles, using maps at any scale. Once you understand the grid, you can give your position, or identify the position of any feature, simply by using a short combination of letters and numbers; in fact, some people who live in remote countryside where street names and house numbers do not apply, often give their location as a grid reference. Youth hostels invariably do this. So, understanding grid references can mean the difference between finding a dry bed for the night, and not. Increasingly, too, people are using GPS co-ordinates to give a precise location, and this is discussed in a later chapter.

Knowing how to give and read grid references is vital in identifying the location of particular 'targets' you will visit – anyone using GPS systems (see 'Walking with map and GPS') can plot these co-ordinates into their GPS receiver – and for giving your location to others. Grid references are a fundamental part of map reading, planning a walk and navigation. There is no mystique about them; they are logical, and easy to use, once they have been understood.

The National Grid

Imagine the whole of Britain covered by a grid of lines where the space between lines in each direction is 100 kilometres – see Figure 4.

In the diagram, each square is 100 kilometres in each direction, and is assigned two letters. There is nothing especially significant for walkers about these letters, but by using them as part of a grid reference it becomes possible to pinpoint (to within 100 kilometres), where a place is. The southern part of the Lake District, for example, is in square 'SD', the northern part in 'NY'; the most westerly part is in 'NX'. The legend on *Explorer* and *Landranger* maps has a small diagram showing any overlap on the map between two or more lettered squares.

Fig. 4: The National Grid

Grid references

The system of assigning letters to squares is the basis of what is known as a **grid reference**.

Of course, being accurate to only 100 kilometres is not good enough

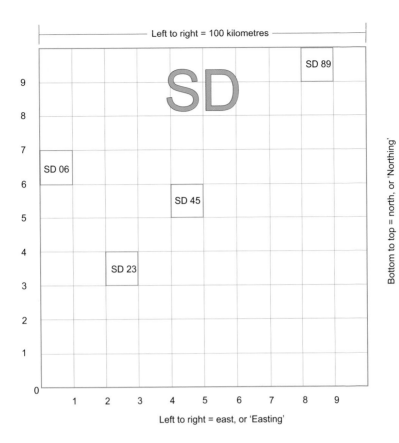

Fig. 5: 100-kilometre grid square, showing 10-kilometre subdivisions

for walking. So, these 100-kilometre squares are further subdivided into smaller squares each representing 10 kilometres. In the above diagram, these 10-kilometre squares are numbered from 0–9 from the bottom left-hand (south-west) corner of the map moving in a left to right (easterly) direction, and from bottom to top (northerly) direction (see Figure 5).

If you look closely at an Ordnance Survey *Explorer* map, along the bottom edge or the sides, at any point that is a multiple of 10, you'll notice that the pale blue lines are a little heavier than the rest. These are the boundaries of the 10-kilometre squares. Because *Explorer* (and other) maps cover areas larger than 10 square kilometres, there is more than one 10-kilometre square (or part of a square) on each map.

> **The technique is to read first from left to right (called 'easting'), and then from bottom to top (called 'northing').**

Using this system you can identify any 10-kilometre grid square, and arrive at a 10-kilometre square grid reference. In Figure 5,

Fig. 6: 10-kilometre grid square, showing 1-kilometre subdivisions

four have been identified – SD06, SD23, SD45 and SD89.

Once numbers come into the grid reference, the location starts to narrow down. The technique is to read first from left to right (this is called 'EASTING'), and then from bottom to top (this is called 'NORTHING').

But this still isn't a sufficient degree of accuracy for walking. It will give a rough position of a feature, a lake, say, that overlaps one or more squares, but for walking, we need to zoom in a bit.

Let's look more closely at a 10-kilometre square: SD45. This is a 10-kilometre square, so, instead of using just '4' and '5', we must allow for the square to be further subdivided. So, we use '40' and '50'. It's the same square, we've just got closer to it – see Figure 6.

Now we can identify squares that are just one kilometre in each direction. In the example above, it is square SD 42 53. If you were on top of a hill on a clear day, you could see from one side of the square to the other. But by using this level of grid reference you could miss your destination by as much as one kilometre. So, we must zoom in another stage, to look more closely at square SD4253.

Fig. 7: The full reference for the illustrated point is SD427537

Once again, if you look at the margins of an *Explorer* map you will notice that between the grid numbers, each one-kilometre square is subdivided, but not numbered – 10 subdivisions in each direction, but only around the borders of the map. This time there are no blue lines on the map. (For a closer look at this see Figure 10, p21.)

Each subdivision now represents just 100 metres, and at this level of accuracy we can arrive at what is called a **six-figure grid reference**, one that gives an accuracy that is adequate for walking purposes.

You can further subdivide: get down to an accuracy of ten metres; this gives an **eight-figure grid reference**, or even an accuracy of one metre, to give a **ten-figure grid reference**. But the reality is that we do not need that level of precision. A six-figure reference, giving an accuracy of 100 metres, is generally good enough.

To arrive at a six-figure grid reference you begin by taking your grid letters (SD, in this example), then a two-figure reference (42), then a four-figure (4253), and finally estimate the one-tenth subdivisions of the 4253 square to arrive as closely as you can at the desired location – see Figure 7 – and remember to read eastings first (west to east/left to right) and then northings (south to north/bottom to top). In this example, the target easting is estimated to be seven-tenths of the distance left to right, and the northing also seven-tenths, but from bottom to top.

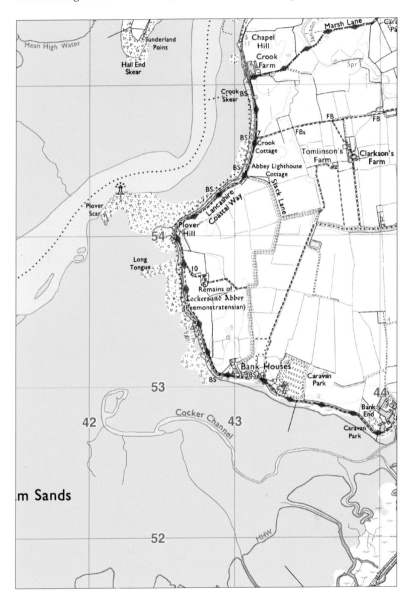

Fig. 8: Extract from OS Explorer Sheet 296, showing location of grid reference
SD427537: Cockersand Abbey

Fig. 9: Having followed the grid referencing this far, here is what Cockersand Abbey looks like today

From this illustration, albeit it in an enlarged state, you can see that should you want greater precision, then you can continue subdividing the squares. But at the scale of maps used for walking, this level of accuracy is difficult to achieve. GPS receivers (about which there is more in the section on 'Information that a GPS device can provide') give a ten-figure grid reference, i.e. to an accuracy of 1m, but, because of the number of satellites and their positions, have an accuracy of only 3–10m at best, which rather makes a nonsense of a ten-figure reference.

In giving grid references in text, it is often useful to prefix everything with the letters 'GR', i.e. GR SD427537, to signify that the number is a grid reference, but the way this appears in print differs from publisher to publisher, and is not vital.

For completeness, the map extract (Figure 8) and picture (Figure 9) show the grid reference we have been working towards: it's Cockersand Abbey, near Lancaster.

Back to the National Grid

Finally, because each National Grid square can be subdivided, it follows that the numbers 427537 will appear in each 100-kilometre square, i.e. at 100-kilometre intervals. This is the reason for using the two letters. By way of illustrating the point, the next northerly use of 427537 is prefixed NY, and locates a street in a housing estate at Harraby on the outskirts of Carlisle. So, for everyday use the letters can be omitted as the six-figure reference will not appear elsewhere on the map in your hand.

The National Grid reference system and OS *Explorer* map legends

Rest assured that should you ever need a reminder of how to use the National Grid reference system, an explanation is given in the map legend on both *Explorer* and *Landranger* maps; see Figure 10.

Figure 10 also shows, in close-up detail, the blue grid, the correspondingly blue 1km grid reference labels for Eastings and Northings, and the 100m subdivisions running around the map border.

THE NATIONAL GRID REFERENCE SYSTEM

The grid lines form part of the national grid and are at 1 km intervals. To give a unique reference position of a point to within 100 metres proceed as follows:

A Read letters identifying 100 000 metre square in which the point lies.

B Locate first VERTICAL grid line to LEFT of point and read LARGE figures labelling the line either in the top or bottom margin or on the line itself. Then estimate tenths from the grid line to point.

C Locate first HORIZONTAL grid line BELOW point and read LARGE figures labelling the line either in the left or right margin or on the line itself. Then estimate tenths from the grid line to point.

EXAMPLE: SD 486 445   For local referencing grid
         A **B** **C**   letters may be omitted.

Fig. 10: Extract from Explorer 296 showing the legend information pertaining to the National Grid reference system

Map legends

Every one of the many maps in the *Landranger* and *Explorer* series produced by Ordnance Survey contains a legend somewhere on the map

Fig. 11: A condensed version of an OS Explorer map legend

HEIGHTS AND NATURAL FEATURES

Water

Mud

Sand

Shingle

Contours are at 5 or 10 metres vertical interval

5m   10m   Vertical face/cliff   Outcrop

Survey height;   Scree   Loose   Boulders
52 · Ground   rock
284 · Air

TOURIST & LEISURE

Camp site

Caravan site

Country park

English Heritage

Golf course or links

Historic Scotland

Information centre (all year)

Information centre (seasonal)

National Trust

Nature reserve

Parking

Picnic site

Public house(s)

Viewpoint

Visitor centre

DANGER AREA Firing and test ranges in the area. Danger! Observe warning notices

MANAGED ACCESS Access permitted within managed controls, for example, local byelaws. gov.uk/guidance/public-access-to-military-areas

PUBLIC RIGHTS OF WAY AND OTHER PUBLIC ACCESS

------- Footpath; public   ------- permissive   Rights of way are liable to change and may not be
— — — Bridleway; public   — — — permissive   clearly defined on the ground.
+ + + Byway open to all traffic   The representation on this map of any other road, track or path is no evidence
+ + Restricted byway   of the existence of a right of way
◆ ◆ Recreational route   ● National Trail   Scotland's Great Trails
● ● Traffic-free cycle route   ● ● Other routes with public access
1 1 National cycle network route number – traffic free; on road

Rights of way are not shown on maps of Scotland, where rights of responsible access apply. For details visit: **outdooraccess-scotland.com**

ACCESS LAND AND COASTAL MARGIN

Access information point   Access land portrayed on this map is intended as a guide to land normally available for access on foot. Some restrictions will apply. Observe local signs and follow the Countryside Code: **gov.uk/government/publications/the-countryside-code**
Access land
– in wooded area
– within sand   All land within the 'coastal margin' (where it already exists) is associated with the England Coast Path (**nationaltrail.co.uk/england-coast-path**).The coastal margin is often steep, unstable and not readily accessible. Please take careful note of conditions and local signage on the ground.
Coastal margin

National Trust for Scotland (NTS)   NTS; limited access
Forestry and Land Scotland   Woodland Trust land

GENERAL FEATURES

Gravel pit   Landfill site or slag/spoil heap
Sand pit
Other pit or quarry   Solar farm
pylon ˙ pole Electricity transmission line
Building; important building
Youth hostel; Bunkhouse or other hostel
Lighthouse, in use; disused
Beacon; Bus station   + Place of worship
Mast; Wind turbine   Current or former place of worship;
Triangulation pillar   with tower
·W; Spr Well; spring   with spire, minaret or dome
Slopes

BOUNDARIES

+ — + — National
— — County
— — — Unitary or District
·········· Civil Parish or Community
▬▬ ▬▬ National Park

VEGETATION

Trees; coniferous, non-coniferous
Coppice
Orchard
Bracken, heath or rough grassland
Scrub
Marsh, reeds or saltings

ROADS AND PATHS   Not necessarily rights of way

M 3
Motorway   Service area   Junction number
A 35
Main road; single, dual carriageway
B 3074
Secondary road
Narrow road with passing places
Road generally more than 4m wide
Road generally less than 4m wide
Other road, drive or track, fenced and unfenced
Path

RAILWAYS

Multiple track } Standard gauge
Single track
Station, open to passengers; siding
Road over; road under; level crossing
Cutting; tunnel; embankment
Narrow gauge, tramway or light rail system; station

For more detailed map information and full legend please visit the Ordnance Survey website; **os.uk** or call **03456 050505**, email **customerservices@os.uk** or its cover. Several examples are given in the pages that follow, and a full list can be viewed, and downloaded, from the Ordnance Survey website (www.ordnancesurvey.co.uk).

A map legend simply defines features that appear on a map; they are visual explanations of the symbols used on maps. Figure 11, shows a condensed version of OS *Explorer* 1:25000 map symbols.

Grouped helpfully into related features such as **communications** (roads and paths, railways, and public rights of way), **general map information** (Access Land, administrative boundaries, specific buildings and man-made features, vegetation types, heights and natural features, and archaeological and historical information), as well as the more familiar pictorial symbols representing **tourist and leisure information**, such as castles, picnic sites and camp sites. They may be simple drawings, a group of letters, shortened words, coloured shapes, or shaded areas. Many of them are self-evident – rivers, roads, vegetation – but they also reflect differences that may not be immediately obvious, and where misunderstanding the differences could have consequences. Examples include appreciating the differences in depiction between a footpath and a bridleway, marsh and rough grassland, and churches with a tower or a spire.

In many instances, knowing whether a church has a tower, or a steeple may not be relevant or important, but if you have one of each in view fairly close together along your route, it helps to know which one you're heading for.

The map legend also appears visually at different scales as a pop-out panel for anyone using the digital *OS Maps*, in both online and app versions. While there are many similarities, the greater amount of detail on 1:25000 maps requires more detailed information than for 1:50000 maps.

On the face of it, the map symbol legend on *Landranger* and *Explorer* maps holds an advantage over *OS Maps*. Opening the legend window in *OS Maps* overlies and obscures the actual mapping. But on the paper maps, the legend may not appear on the side or fold-out of the map you are using – not a problem on a fine day, but potentially troublesome if you have to unfold and refold maps in windy conditions.

It's worth spending time studying map legends, and, to begin with, identifying the features and the shorthand symbols for them that you are most likely to need: if you are walking in the Yorkshire Dales, it's unlikely you'll need to know the difference between an operational lighthouse and a non-operational one. But walk along the coast of Britain, and a lighthouse might be significant in following a route to your desired location.

It all may seem confusing, but the vast amount of information that these legends convey make reading maps an intriguing and fascinating activity.

Understanding contours

Contours are wonderful: they tell you so much more about the terrain you're proposing to walk into than perhaps anything else on a map. Most importantly, they tell you whether the landscape is flat, undulating, hilly or too steep even to think about. But they are tricky little things, and need a bit of time to understand them properly.

Put simply, a contour is an imaginary line (they appear only on maps, sadly) that joins up all the points on the ground that are of the same height. What contours by themselves do not tell us is whether the land is going up or going down. To get this information, we need other clues: two in particular. One is the relationship between the contours – which are higher, which are lower. In other words, we need to know the height of the contours. The other big clue is rivers and streams, since, thanks to gravity, they flow downwards. Unfortunately, even in a wet country like Britain, there are a few places where there are no rivers and streams: then we have to rely on contours.

Contour intervals

Fig. 12: Contour interval extract from Explorer 296 map legend

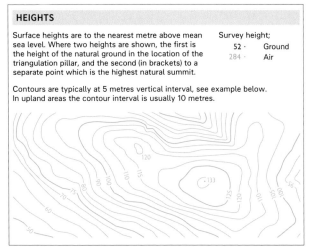

Contours are shown on maps as reddish-brown lines spaced vertically at regular intervals. The marginal data on maps tells you what this interval is: it's called the **vertical interval**. See Figure 12.

On maps to

a scale of 1:25000, the vertical interval is usually five metres on lowland maps and ten metres on upland maps. On 1:50000 maps it is usually ten metres. Take a moment to check the interval on the map you are using.

On some old maps of Ireland, the vertical interval was a massive 50 metres. A lot can happen in 50 metres, and the effect was to give the impression that all the hills in Ireland had flat tops. Of course they do not, but you need more refined vertical intervals to give a better idea of the shape of the land.

The height of contour lines

The height of contour lines is given on maps, but problems of space mean that not every contour line can be given a height. However, if you know the vertical interval you can easily count the lines from a numbered line and arrive at the correct height for any given contour. You just need to know whether you're counting up or down.

The height of contour lines is printed so that the top of the number points uphill.

The horizontal spacing of contours is variable depending on the nature of the landscape. Flat terrain will have the contours spaced widely apart; steep terrain will have them close together.

To make life a little easier, every fifth contour line is darker and stronger than the others. What isn't instantly obvious, until you study maps a little more, is that the height of contour lines is always printed so that the top of the number is pointing uphill.

Interpreting contours

There are few places in Britain that are totally devoid of some form of man-made feature (see 'Landscape features', p38), but they may be widely spread, or obscured by dips in the landscape or by mist. So, the ability to read contours is, as the next

Fig. 13: Is it a hill or a hole?

illustration shows, vital.

Take a look at Figure 13 – it's actually of Great Mell Fell in the Lake District. Without the contour heights, while you might imagine that this is a hill, you could equally be looking into a chasm.

Moreover, this diagram also serves to illustrate that the closer the contour lines in a horizontal relationship, the steeper the terrain.

Now consider Figure 14. This shows three samples of contour line grouping. In all cases, the contour lines descend from left to right (for illustration purposes only).

Fig. 14: Contour lines

(A) Straight slope

(B) Concave slope

(C) Convex slope

Where the contours are evenly spaced, then the slope is uniform (A). In (B) the contour lines are closer together on the left, and this denotes what is called a concave slope. Example (C) shows the contours more closely grouped on the right; this illustrates a convex slope.

Of course, things are not so simple in reality, and hill slopes are often a mix of all three types. Understanding these three basic slope types, as depicted by contours on a map, will help when it comes to planning a walk, and in navigation.

Spot heights

Dotted all over maps are numbers in small print. These are spot heights, i.e. heights that have been surveyed to the nearest metre above mean sea level. There are two types. Those shown in black are 'ground survey' heights; those in brown are 'air survey' heights (look back to Figure 12, p24). As a rule, up to 80 per cent of ground detail is collected using aerial

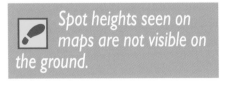

Spot heights seen on maps are not visible on the ground.

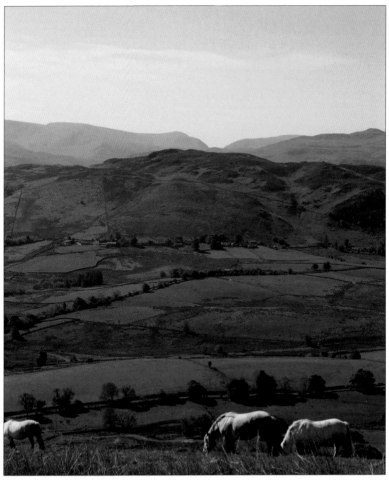

Indisputably a hill; the wonderful view from Great Mell Fell

photography, but this is not always possible because shadows, clouds, tree cover and overhanging eaves on buildings mean that the surveyor still has to carry out surveys on the ground.

A height shown close by a trig pillar (about which more in 'Landscape features', p39) refers to the ground level height at the pillar; it does not necessarily refer to the height of a mountain or hill summit. Trig pillars are often (but not always) on the summit of hills, but that is not their reason for being there, and the need to use them to take accurate measurements meant that they were positioned where it was most convenient for surveys to be carried out.

One key thing to remember is that while trig pillars are visible, spot heights are not, and no reliance should be placed on them for navigational purposes. You will not find a spot height on the ground.

Access: roads, tracks, footpaths, bridleways and Access Land

For the purposes of this chapter reference is made mainly to Ordnance Survey *Explorer* maps and the digital *OS Maps*, and the information they contain.

A map is simply a representation on paper of an area of terrain, a bird's-eye view, in fact. But unlike a bird's-eye view or aerial photograph, which shows everything visible, a map is selective. Map-makers choose what information to put on a map, notably those objects likely to be of interest to the people for whom the map is intended, like paths, roads, streams, rivers and bridges. These are represented diagrammatically: a barn is not depicted with a sloping roof, nor necessarily at a precise size – on small-scale maps this simply isn't possible – but by means of a small rectangle. The position of features on maps is likely to be remarkably accurate, but in terms of relative size, they may be exaggerated – roads and footpaths, for example, are wider on a scale map than they are in real life.

This technique is a kind of shorthand used by cartographers. But so that you understand the keys that the map-maker is using, all this information, about paths and buildings, roads and streams is annotated somewhere on the map, generally in one large panel adjacent to it (see Map legends', p22).

So, let's take a look at the most directly relevant symbols that you'll need to recognise and understand; we can return to the others later. The following are all taken from the *Explorer* series of maps.

Roads and tracks

Other than motorways, you can walk on roads. They are open to all traffic. Busy main roads, however, are not fun to walk along, although it may be necessary to include them in a walk for short stretches. But many of the minor roads are a delight to walk, and make for speedy (or unhurried, leisurely) progress.

To make life easy, the different classes of roads are colour-coded on maps (see Figure 15).

Motorways are shown in blue; main roads in red. Secondary roads, the B-roads, are brown. The map legend even differentiates between

Fig. 15: Roads and tracks as depicted on Ordnance Survey maps

ROADS AND PATHS   Not necessarily rights of way

M 3	Motorway **S** Service area **7** Junction number
A 35	Main road; single, dual carriageway
B 3074	Secondary road
═══	Narrow road with passing places
═══	Road generally more than 4m wide
═══	Road generally less than 4m wide
═╌╌	Other road, drive or track, fenced and unfenced
·········	Path

roads over or under four metres in width. Those less than four metres wide are depicted in yellow, and these are the roads most usually found in rural locations.

Look closely at the map, however, and you may pick out that while most roads have a solid line on both sides of them, some do not, or have a dotted line. A solid line tells you that the road is either fenced or has a wall beside it (on one or both sides); a dotted line signifies that the road is unenclosed. These are customarily found across common land or open upland pastures to which there is a traditional and long-standing right of free access.

Roads in housing estates are invariably shown as white, but out in the countryside there are other so-called 'white roads' (see Figure 16). These can be anything from a surfaced lane to a private drive; maybe they depict the course of an old 'green lane' or an ancient packhorse route.

Fig. 16: Walled 'white road' – an 'Occupation' road – across Twiston Moor, Pendle

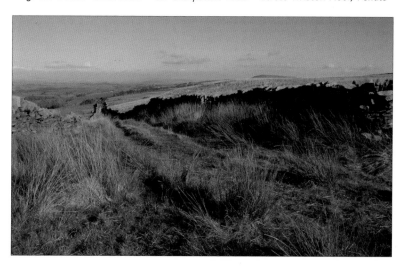

Sometimes they may be what are known as 'Occupation' roads, i.e. service tracks for the flanking landowners, along which they drive sheep or cattle and farm vehicles. These are splendid to walk, but whether you can do so legally is not information found on maps. That's a pity because they often have a sense of history about them, and connect other, legitimate, routes.

So, how do you find out? With some, the position is clear. If you encounter a white road with green dots along it, then the road is an 'unclassified county road', which you can walk along. All others are private. Often, walkers are tolerated along these; many have been thoroughfares for centuries. But the only sure way to find out is when you arrive on one: if there is a 'Private' sign, then you need an alternative route to switch to. You may get away with walking white roads, but that's all you are doing – getting away with it: you cannot be certain that you are walking the route lawfully.

Footpaths and bridleways

Until what has become known as 'Access Land' was created in England and Wales under the *Countryside and Rights of Way Act 2000 (CROW)*, when you walked in the countryside you were confined to using public rights of way, many of which have their roots in long-established pedestrian (and other) routes across the countryside.

> There is a point of view that rights of way provide freedom of access to the countryside; there is another view that they are actually restrictions on freedom because walkers are confined to the course of the path.

The situation was slightly different in Scotland. Walkers in Scotland have long enjoyed a moral and de facto right of access. Nothing much has changed except that this is now enshrined in *The Land Reform (Scotland) Act 2003*. The Act tells you where you have right of access and *The Scottish Outdoor Access Code* sets out your responsibilities when exercising your rights. These rights came into effect in February 2005.

Footpaths on maps are denoted by a black dotted line, as seen in Figure 15, but they are simply that – a footpath, and not necessarily a lawful right of way. Where rights of way exist along a footpath, they are shown on Ordnance Survey *Explorer* maps in green, and are properly described as 'Public footpaths' (see Figure 17). In Scotland, where the rights of way system is different and less developed than in England and Wales, public footpaths and bridleways are not shown in green, but are depicted as a black dashed line instead.

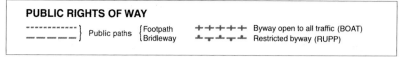

PUBLIC RIGHTS OF WAY

} Public paths {Footpath ++++++ Byway open to all traffic (BOAT)
                 Bridleway   Restricted byway (RUPP)

Fig. 17: Footpath, bridleway, BOATs and RUPPs as depicted on Ordnance Survey maps

The terms 'public right of way' and 'highway' both mean a way over which the public have a right to pass and re-pass. There is a distinction, however, in that a 'right' is an abstract thing, while a 'highway' is in essence a strip of land. The nature of the right determines the type of way, which can be either:

- a **footpath** (marked on maps by small green dashes) over which the right of way is on foot only; or

- a **bridleway** (marked by larger green dashes) over which the right of way is on foot and on horseback.

In 1968, Parliament granted cyclists the right to use bridleways, and also introduced the notion of cycle tracks (see page 33) over which there is a right to cycle, and possibly also to walk.

In addition to footpaths and bridleways, which are the principal routes for the enjoyment of walking, there are two other categories depicted on Ordnance Survey maps:

- **Byway Open to All Traffic (BOAT)**: this is a special category (shown on maps as a line of small green elongated crosses). BOATs are

Fig. 18: The national network of rights of way

Composition of the national network

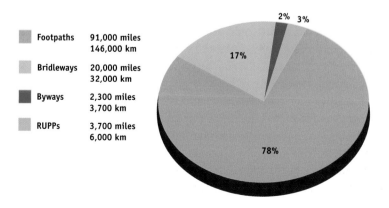

Footpaths	91,000 miles	146,000 km
Bridleways	20,000 miles	32,000 km
Byways	2,300 miles	3,700 km
RUPPs	3,700 miles	6,000 km

technically carriageways, and so a right of way for vehicular traffic, but used mainly for the purposes for which footpaths and bridleways are used, namely, by walkers and horse-riders.

- **Road Used as a Public Path** (RUPP): this is exactly what it is (shown on maps as a line of alternating flattened green 'T's). RUPPs are 'restricted byways' over which the public has a right of way for vehicles other than mechanically propelled vehicles, so giving a right of way on foot, on horseback or leading a horse, and for cyclists.

Figure 18 shows the relative incidence of each of the above rights of way in England.

Most of the rights of way encountered on a walk are either public footpaths or bridleways, but while maps depict them, there is no guarantee that they actually exist on the ground. Many will have become overgrown or blocked, and there is really only one way to find out – you have to walk them, and be prepared to make changes to your plans.

Other routes with public access

In addition to the green-coloured rights of way, you find other symbols and colours that show where you may walk, but the exact nature in law, and any restrictions that apply to them, is often variable.

- **Permissive or concessionary paths and bridleways** (depicted in orange) are not rights of way, but show the course of routes for public use where the path has been negotiated with the landowner, but with the intention that they should never become rights of way. Because they are permissive, they can be closed, and the landowner may erect notices to that effect and, indeed, close them on at least one day a year to ensure that the public does not acquire a right of way. In practice, permissive routes provide missing links in the path network, and often lead to places of special interest or outstanding viewpoints.

- **National trails and long-distance routes** (depicted by green diamond-shaped lozenges) are recreational routes. Usually they follow existing rights of way, and the diamond symbol serves simply to mark the line of the route. Occasionally, however, they are not over defined rights of way, but along routes where permission to walk already exists, or is given. In such cases, the alignment shown on maps is no more than the best information available, and may have on-the-ground variations. You should use common sense when dealing with them, and observe any diversion signs.

- **Other routes** (depicted by a line of green dots) are usually found overlying white roads. They are a clear indication that you can use a white road for walking. The same symbol, but in orange, denotes a traffic-free cycle route; you can walk these, too. The expression cycle track has various meanings. In one sense, it can mean a way over which cyclists have a legal right of passage along with other users, such as bridleways. It can also mean a way over which cyclists can pass, usually along with others, by permission of the landowner – certain sections of the routes promoted by SUSTRANS (a charity promoting sustainable transport), and the Monsal Trail in the Peak District, fall into this category. In some areas, the expression means a way over which cyclists have exclusive right of passage. It can also be used to describe a public footpath that has been converted to a cycle track under the provisions of the Cycle Tracks Act 1984.

Access Land

The *Countryside and Rights of Way Act 2000* gives a public right of access to land mapped as open country (mountain, moor, heath and down) or registered common land. These areas are known as 'open access land', and include land around the coastline, known as coastal margin.

Fig. 19: England Coast Path and Coastal Access depiction

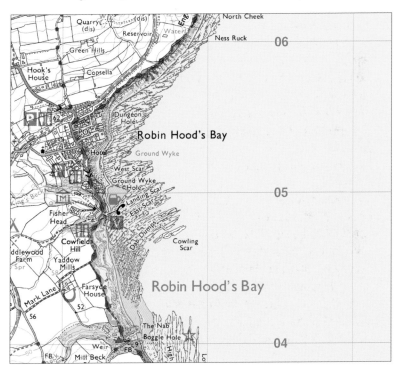

A **coastal margin** (depicted on OS *Explorer* mapping as shown in Figure 19) is part of the work to implement the England Coast Path (ECP), a proposed long-distance National Trail which will follow the coastline of England, and being implemented by Natural England. When complete, it will run for 2,795 miles (4,500 kilometres). The England Coast Path has been possible because of a new law in the UK, the 'Right of Coastal Access', giving to people for the first time the right of access around all England's open coast, both along the ECP and, usually, over the associated 'coastal margin'. There is a corresponding Wales Coast Path, but as yet there isn't a Scottish Coast Path. However, the right to responsible access to land allows people to access Scotland's entire coastline, and so there is no bar to a person wishing to walk the length of the coastline.

Coastal access rights apply within the coastal margin (including along the coast path itself) unless the land falls into a category of excepted land or is subject to local restrictions, exclusions or diversions.

Walking on Access Land provides the chance to explore huge areas of the countryside without resorting to paths of any kind or rights of way. Commonly known as the 'Right to Roam', this right covers some of the most wild and dramatic landscapes. 'Access Land' is depicted on Ordnance Survey maps by a pale orange/brown tint, surrounded by a stronger orange/brown line. Access Land in woodlands is shaded green, as in Figure 20.

Within Access Land you can wander at will; whether you would

Fig. 20: Example of boundaries of Access Land, and the distinctive shading used for Access Land in woodlands. Notice the different types of woodland shown on this extract

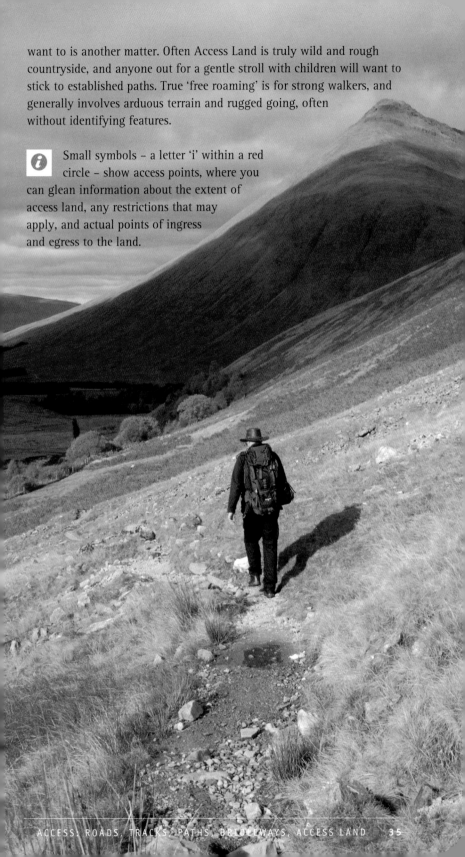

want to is another matter. Often Access Land is truly wild and rough countryside, and anyone out for a gentle stroll with children will want to stick to established paths. True 'free roaming' is for strong walkers, and generally involves arduous terrain and rugged going, often without identifying features.

Small symbols – a letter 'i' within a red circle – show access points, where you can glean information about the extent of access land, any restrictions that may apply, and actual points of ingress and egress to the land.

Landscape features: natural and man-made

One of the joys of walking in the UK is the exhilaration of striding out over wild, uncultivated moorland. It is one of the freedoms for which campaigners fought in the late 19th century – the struggle for access to the moors around Darwen and Bolton in 1896 – and almost 40 years later (1932) the more widely known trespass on Kinder Scout. For many years, when walkers enjoyed the open moors it was along existing public rights of way; all that changed when the provisions of the Countryside and Rights of Way Act 2000 (CROW) came into force. Under the Act, the public may walk freely on mapped areas of mountain, moor, heath, down, coast and registered land without the need to stick to paths.

Understanding of rights of way, permissive paths and Access Land does not, however, provide enough information to enable you to plan a successful walk. Nothing so far mentioned says anything about the 'lie of the land'. Being able to recognise the many and varied landscape features will enable you to plot an enjoyable route.

There is a huge amount of information on a map, yet few newcomers to map reading take the time to study the detail. As a result, they fail to comprehend what the map is telling them, and how this information can be used to help with route planning and with navigation.

Take time to study the map.

Natural features

Vegetation

Large expanses of sheep-cropped turf are a delight to walk, but there are other types of vegetation that can make progress a less agreeable experience. Equally, bluebell-filled woodlands in springtime are a delight, except that the maps do not tell you about the bluebells, just the woodland.

The marginal data on maps shows the types of vegetation that can be found, distinguishing between coniferous and non-coniferous trees, coppiced woodland and orchards. Scrub, heath, saltings, reed beds, rough grassland and bracken are also depicted on maps, and give you some idea of the sort of terrain likely to be encountered (see Figure 21).

What the maps cannot show is the condition or density of the

Fig. 21: Vegetation types as shown on Ordnance Survey maps

VEGETATION   Limits of vegetation are defined by positioning of symbols

Coniferous trees	Scrub	Bracken, heath or rough grassland
Non-coniferous trees	Orchard	Marsh, reeds or saltings
Coppice		

vegetation. Coniferous plantations are often dark, tightly packed, gloomy and impassable; oak and beech woodlands are not – oak and beech just won't grow so closely together. So, you might want to avoid coniferous plantations, but be happy enough to tackle a route through an oak woodland. Notice that distinction between 'plantation' and 'woodland': the former is generally used to signify a commercial planting of trees, whereas a 'woodland', while possibly also planted, is likely to be more natural and pleasurable, and often truly native. Where the two occur, often broad-leaved trees and larch, for example, this is referred to as 'mixed woodland'.

For anyone following a route across country, woodlands and plantations are valuable aids to navigation. They have fairly regular and uniform boundaries, sometimes fenced, sometimes unfenced (as with roads), no two woodlands have the same shape, and they enable you to pinpoint exactly your position on the map.

Of course woodlands, and more frequently, plantations are felled and cleared; sometimes new ones are planted. But thankfully the rate of this activity is slow enough for it to have little serious impact on the accuracy of a map; even with a recently cleared plantation, you can see where it has been for many years afterwards.

Rivers and streams

Depicted by blue lines with a thickness that roughly approximates to their width, rivers and streams feature on every one of the *Explorer* series of maps. Crossing points are usually shown either as a footbridge (FB), a 'Ford' or as 'Stepping Stones'. But it is not safe to assume that simply because a footpath runs down to a stream and continues on the other side there is necessarily a 'dry' crossing point. Fords can be of varying depth, and sometimes impassable. Nor are stepping stones wholly reliable. Often they may be under water, and seldom is it that they are uniformly flat, allowing walkers to step easily across. Quite frequently one or more of the stones becomes dislodged, leaving you with an uncomfortable step or jump to complete the crossing, and, in some instances, no way across at all.

If you look closely at a 1:25000 map you can see if the green footpath line has solid black lines on both sides. In this case, there is likely to be some secure form of crossing but otherwise, it can be a guessing game with a damp answer.

Lakes and reservoirs
Water is depicted on maps in pale blue surrounded by a deep blue line. It is quite obvious which areas are lakes, but a little less obvious which are reservoirs. The give-away with reservoirs, although not always so, is a straight edge to the 'lake' where the dam has been formed. The vicinity of many lakes and reservoirs are now open to walkers, and provide a key focal point to enjoyment of the countryside.

Crags, loose rock, boulders, outcrop and scree
These various forms of landscape feature will almost certainly have an influence on route planning, and need to be recognised. There are differing symbols for each (see Figure 22), but all should be thought of at best as arduous and dangerous terrain, and at worst a 'no go' zone ideally to be avoided. Many parts of Britain are, however, craggy, and, for many, desirable places to be.

The symbols for crags, loose rock, boulders, outcrop and scree should be regarded as a warning that, combined with other map symbols and information, determine whether it is somewhere safe to walk.

Fig. 22: Symbols for crags, loose rock, boulders, outcrop and scree as depicted on Ordnance Survey maps

Man-made features
Field boundaries
Maps are draped with thousands of field boundaries, shown as thin black lines. What the map cannot show is whether the boundary is a wall, fence or a hedgerow, or what size the wall, hedge or fence is.

Maps do not indicate how such boundaries might be crossed. If a footpath is indicated crossing a field boundary, there will be some form of crossing point – one of the numerous forms of stile, as a rule, but not all of them are accommodating of persons of generous girth (see Figure 23).

As land use changes, so field boundaries disappear, but it is often a long time before they disappear from maps. There are instances of field boundaries shown on maps that were physically removed more than 40 years ago. From a practical point of view all that this does is generate the need to be aware that field boundaries may have gone. It is an easy thing to become confused if an expected (and depicted) field boundary is no longer

Fig. 23: Boundaries and stiles can vary greatly on the ground

Grubbed out field boundary along-side old green track

Stone gap stile – a tight squeeze

there on the ground. But an awareness that this sort of thing happens helps; quite often you can still see where the original boundary lay.

In spite of these inherent difficulties, field boundaries are one of the surest forms of navigation. There are few boundaries that are straight, and these in-built bends and sudden changes of direction are a great help in both determining where exactly you are, and in spotting the boundaries that are missing.

Triangulation pillars

Popularly known as 'trig' pillars, these obelisks of surveying days of old are a part of our heritage, much loved especially by walkers who may be temporarily misplaced in their travels and then suddenly find one, and, above all else, a clear and precise indication of an exact location. All trig pillars have been very accurately surveyed, and Ordnance Survey archives contain details of their position and height to many decimal places. In poor visibility, they are crucial. On maps they are identified by a small blue triangle with a dot at its centre.

These days the Ordnance Survey uses satellites to fix positions, making the familiar trig pillars obsolete. But they have been around for many years, and it will be a long time before they disappear from our landscape, if at all. Each one carries a specific identifying number in a brass plate near its base. Walkers have been known to annotate maps with the identification number of trig pillars visited; if nothing else, it proves you were there.

In winter conditions, on bleak moorland, isn't it good to know exactly where you are? This is a trig pillar at Gragareth – the highest summit in Lancashire

Buildings

Generally, buildings are shown on maps as small rectangles that approximate, as near as they reasonably can, to the size and shape of the real thing. They are almost invariably in exactly the correct position, i.e. they are not randomly placed onto the map. So, you can rely on them for navigational purposes.

Farm buildings and field barns are the most common buildings represented by a rectangle. But if you look at the legend on the map border you will see that some buildings have very specific symbols – churches, other places of worship, youth hostels, bunkhouses, camping barns, lighthouses and windmills – Figure 24.

All are very useful, but among these, three symbols are especially effective in helping to

Fig. 24: Building symbols

i	Place	with tower
i	of	with spire, minaret or dome
+	worship	without such additions
▲		Youth hostel
▮		Bunkhouse/camping barn/other hostel
Ӑ ʇ ⅄		Lighthouse; disused lighthouse; beacon
Ӿ		Windmill, with or without sails

find your way when out on a walk. These are the symbols for places of worship, and there are three kinds (also see 'Map legends', p22):

- A **church with a tower** is shown in black as a small cross on top of a square. Think of the square as a squat tower, and you'll never be confused.

- A **church with a steeple** is shown in black as a small cross on top of a circle. The 'think square, think tower' suggestion does not work with steeples. But, if it's not a tower, it must be a steeple.

- A **chapel or a church with neither** a tower nor a steeple is shown in black as a small cross.

As long established features of our British countryside, churches are wonderful navigational aids.

There is another interesting point about churches that can help with orientation. Most (but not all) churches are built on an east-west alignment, usually with the tower or steeple at the western end.

Distance and heights

Fig. 25: Holcombe Moor walk, from OS Pathfinder Guide Lancashire

Calculating distance by using a map is not an exact science. Nor can it be. Given that a map is a scaled-down view of things, it follows that the level of accuracy, when measuring distances, is limited. But it rarely matters that in a walk of, say 10km, you need to be accurate to a few metres. What you may need to know is whether the distance you have to walk is 9, 10 or 11 kilometres, because this will affect how long it will take you to complete the route.

Rough and ready

What makes measuring distance really easy is that the map is already conveniently overlain with a measuring device – the grid, and each square represents one kilometre. Take a look at the map extract in Figure 25.

> *To roughly convert kilometres to miles, multiply by 0.6, then round up. 16 kilometres x 0.6 = 9.6 miles, near enough.*

With such a ready guide, it is comparatively easy to roughly measure distance. Allowing for the various kinks and bends in the route, but using the one-kilometre grid as a guide, you can roughly calculate the walk to be around 7km (the guidebook gives 7.3km). In fact, when measured more accurately using *OS Maps* digital mapping resource, the walk is 7.25km. So, the rough calculation was easily good enough.

Once you get used to this technique, you become more adept at making these rough calculations. And the beauty is, it works at any scale. Just use the grid squares as a guide. This simple technique is by no means scientifically accurate, but neither is it disastrously inaccurate. Rough measuring like this can be critical should you need to vary a route mid-walk in an emergency or for other reasons.

A word of caution

There is another relatively minor issue concerning the measurement of distance to introduce at this stage. In fact, there are two variations on the same issue.

First, if you are using the one kilometre grid square to measure distance, you need to understand that it only measures one kilometre horizontally and vertically. Those adept at geometry will instantly understand, but take a look at the illustration (Figure 26).

Fig 26: Kilometre grid square

It's simple Pythagoras. It just means that the distance across the diagonal is 40 per cent more than horizontally or vertically.

Second, if you measure a distance of one kilometre on a map, then, if the land is flat, one kilometre is the actual distance you have to travel. On the other hand, if the kilometre is across steep or undulating terrain, then the distance is going to be a little farther.

If the ground is flat then the distance between A and B will be as measured. But if the ground is steep, as in Figure 27, then the distance from A to B will be longer. On a short walk the difference will be negligible; you just need to be aware of it. If A to B is 3,000 metres, and the height difference 400 metres, then the actual distance walked is 3,026.5 metres. But repeat that over a much longer walk, and you can see that the 'invisible' extra distance can amount to something to be reckoned with.

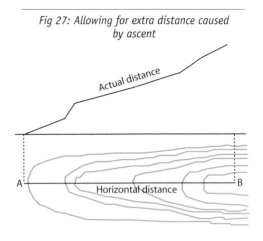

Fig 27: Allowing for extra distance caused by ascent

OS Maps

The digital mapping portal provided by Ordnance Survey – *OS Maps* – is a boon. More is explained about this system below, but it provides the ability to plot a route on a digital map on your desktop or handheld device, enabling you to calculate the distance of a walk as accurately as possible, with information about the total ascent involved. The larger the scale at which the route is plotted, the more intermediate points can be inserted, and the more accurate will be the final calculation.

This conveniently leads into calculating ascent and descent, rather than distance.

Fig. 28: A route card displayed in OS Maps with details of the walk distance, ascent, descent and an elevation profile

Calculating height

To find the height of a feature by looking at the map, you need to find the nearest contour line to it that has a value, or use a nearby spot height (see page 26) if there is one. If you are using a spot height, remember that the given height is of the spot and not a contour line.

Consider Figure 29 above, and imagine that you want to calculate the height of Rae Crags (GR 334343). The crags are on a bold contour line, but, inconveniently in this case, it doesn't have a height label close by. The nearest number is 600 metres; the top of the number points up hill, remember. So, Rae Crags are lower than 600 metres.

The extract in Figure 29 is from a 1:25000 map, and the contour interval on upland maps is 10 metres. Count the number of contour lines down to Rae Crags: five. Multiply by the contour interval, 10 metres (50 metres), and subtract from 600, to put Rae Crags on the 550-metre contour line.

If you want to check that you've done this correctly, there is another spot height (323) near

GR 345348. The interval between the bold contour lines is 50 metres, so count down from the 600-metre contour. The bold contour line just above the spot height is 350 metres, and the spot height between two and three single contour lines lower down, i.e. between 330 metres and 320 metres. Of course, you could just as easily have used the spot height, 323, to count up to Rae Crags.

The nature of the landscape often means that contour heights cannot always be given uniformly across the map, so you do need to recognise that sometimes you'll be counting up to a height, and sometimes down.

Calculating height difference

Height difference is just that: the difference between two heights. Go back to Figure 29. The height difference between spot height 323 and Rae Crags (550 metres) is simple subtraction – 227 metres.

But what is the height difference between spot height 323 and the summit of Carrock Fell? The danger here is that you are lulled by spot height 649, near the top of Carrock Fell, into thinking that marks the summit of the fell. But look more closely. The actual digits 649 sit on the 640 metre contour line (the dot that is the spot height point is difficult to make out) and there is a bold contour line above that. This is 650 metres. And if you look even more closely you'll find a tiny circular contour line above that, which must be 660 metres. So, the top of Carrock Fell must be higher than 660 metres, and not 649 metres as the spot height might tempt you into thinking. The actual height is 661 metres, but you cannot see that on 1:25000 maps because the bit of Carrock Fell that reaches up to 661 metres is too tiny to figure on maps at that scale.

So, the height difference between spot height 323 and the top of Carrock Fell using the information from the 1:25000 map is 337+ metres, but in fact 338 metres if you know the correct height for Carrock Fell.

Calculating height difference in this way is straightforward, but all it does is tell you just that, the difference between two heights. If the two heights are separated by a continually rising slope then the height difference is the amount of climbing you will have to do. But it is not necessarily the same as the amount of height you would have to climb on a walk with numerous ups and downs.

Calculating height gain goes one step further.

Calculating height gain

Height gain is the amount of height you have to climb on a walk, and is the sum total of all the up sections, not just the difference between the starting point and the highest

To convert metres to feet, multiply by 3.3.

summit. Conversely, height loss is the sum of all the down sections. Figure 30 illustrates the point.

Fig. 30: Height gain is the sum of the height difference at each of the three points A, B and C

Direction of walk ⟶

Now look at Figure 31, and let's assume you want to calculate the height gain involved in walking from High Pike to Carrock Fell along the route marked.

Fig. 31: Calculating height gain

The first thing to recognise is that there are certain known heights – those of summits:

High Pike 658
Hare Stones 627
Miton Hill 607
Round Knott 603
Carrock Fell 661

There are other known heights, too, namely those that are spot heights:
611, south of High Pike (Point Z)
572, west of Miton Hill (Point Y)

But some intermediate heights – those marked on the map with a red circle – are not known. In this example, they are not hugely significant, but if you imagined a height difference of several hundred metres between each of the known and unknown points on the map, you begin to see why it becomes important to bring these unknown heights into the equation.

So, what can you do? The only answer is to arrive at a best estimate. Let's consider each in turn:

Point A – lies between the 600 metre contour on Carrock Fell and the 600 metre contour on Round Knott. The contour lines to the north and south of this point are 590 metres. So, Point A lies between 590 metres and 600 metres. The only reasonable option is to call Point A 595metres.

Point B – is exactly the same, for the same reasons, 595 metres.

Point C – lies between the 620 metres contour on Drygill Head, and the 620 metres contour on Hare Stones. The next lowest contour line is 610 metres. So, Point C becomes 615 metres.

Now the only other unknown height is that of Drygill Head. In reality you would not visit Drygill Head, but use that track just to the north of it; it is included here for demonstration purposes. Drygill Head is higher than 620 metres. There are no more contour rings. The next contour up would have been 630 metres. So, you make an assumption: Drygill Head is 625 metres.

To complete the calculation you must do some adding and subtracting.

To begin you can ignore the height of High Pike, as we are descending from it. In fact, you can ignore all the descents, unless you want to know that information too.

The calculation for height gain starts at Point Z – 611 metres. Now:
Ascend to Hare Stones (627) = 16 metres
Point C (615) to Drygill Head (625) = 10 metres
Point Y (572) to Miton Hill (607) = 35 metres
Point B (595) to Round Knott (603) = 8 metres
Point A (595) to Carrock Fell (661) = 66 metres

The total height gain then is 135 metres. Had you simply taken the height difference between Point Z and the top of Carrock Fell the answer would have been just 50 metres which is quite different.

Going in the opposite direction, from Carrock Fell to High Pike, the height gain is 132 metres. See if you can work it out for yourself.

Does this system work everywhere?

Unfortunately, there are places where calculating height gain in this manner is just impossible. Look at the map below (Figure 32). It shows a section of the Cuillin Ridge on the Isle of Skye, a stretch of mountainous countryside so complex there simply is not room for the information needed to help calculate height gain.

Fig. 32: Cuillin Ridge, Isle of Skye

The last word

In the above illustrations, the start and finish heights were different places. So, height gain and the amount of descent (height loss) would be different. But if you start and finish at exactly the same spot, the height gain and height loss are equal, regardless of which way you travel.

Interpreting relief and terrain

Perhaps the most important skill to be learned at an early stage is to understand what the map is telling you; what kind of terrain you are looking at. First impressions often tell you a lot, but then you need to study the map in greater detail. It may look confusing, but a map is a treasure trove of information, and understanding what the information on the map is saying will better equip you to deal with situations on the ground.

Fig. 33: Extract from Explorer OL5, showing Kidsty Pike and Riggindale, Lake District

A sense of relief

We can look at two examples. Figure 33 (above) shows a rugged part of the Lake District; Figure 36 on page 53, shows an extract from the Chilterns, quite a different landscape picture.

What does the Lake District extract say about the landscape?

First impressions:

- closely packed contour lines that indicate steep slopes

- some less steep ground, shown by the more spaced-out contour lines. This is upland, so the contour interval is 10 metres

- streams and lakes

- quite a lot of craggy and bouldery terrain

- a few rights of way, but that is not so much a problem because the strong brown line along the edge of the lake (actually Haweswater Reservoir) shows that this is mainly Access Land.

A closer look shows:

- the land is falling west to east; you can tell that by the contour heights leading up to Kidsty Pike

- the highest ground is in the west, around High Street

- there are few clearly defined summits; most are simply rounded uplifts above the adjacent land

- north of High Street a gentle slope is flanked by very steep ground. This is a descending **ridge**, and leads north to a very narrow neck of land, a **saddle**, called the Straits of Riggindale

- from the saddle, the land to the north-west descends irregularly around The Knott, although the western slope of High Street, as it falls to Hayeswater, is quite uniform

- from the saddle, the land to the north-east actually climbs around the rim of the valley to the east, Riggindale

- a very narrow ridge runs from Mardale Head almost exactly east–west to the top of High Street. This is Rough Crag; the name should also tell you something. The ridge is very narrow, with tightly packed contour lines pressing in from the north and south; it is also rocky on both flanks

- although the Rough Crag ridge has a right of way shown along it, if you look closely you can see the dashed line of a path, which initially sets off from the east by keeping to the south of a boundary (a wall, in fact). Since the marked right of way seems to tangle with some rocky ground to the north of the wall, you might reasonably expect to find yourself on the dotted path rather than the right of way. In fact, the right of way is virtually unwalkable; attempting it is not recommended. But it is worth making the point here that religiously sticking to the course of a 'green' right of way is not always the best plan. Look closely at the map; do not make assumptions, or you may have assumed that the path along Rough Crag was to the north of the wall, when, in fact, it's to the south. That can make quite a difference in poor visibility

- the ridge of Rough Crag becomes very steep as it adjoins High Street, to the west of the tiny pond at Caspel Gate
- the **height difference** between the starting point at Mardale Head and High Street summit is 576 metres. Of course that is not the same as **height gain**; there is a slight descent from the top of Rough Crag to Caspel Gate, and likewise from Kidsty Pike to the Straits of Riggindale, and this will affect your calculations.

If High Street was your objective, you might prefer to consider the rather easier option over Kidsty Pike. Certainly the gradient looks a lot more manageable, but it is clearly farther to walk. This is where you start weighing up all of the above information to decide on the route you would take.

'Planning a walk' is covered in the next chapter; suffice to say here that the best circuit to make would be up Rough Crag first to High Street, then north and round to Kidsty Pike, then descending from there. Unfortunately, this sort of information is not found on maps because it introduces other dimensions – pleasure, effort and reward – a rugged and energetic start to a major summit, followed by a more relaxed descent. Perfect.

These two pictures show some of the terrain in question. Figure 34 is looking down into Riggindale – that deeply incised valley between the ridge of Rough Crag on the right, and the slopes rising to Kidsty Pike on the left.

Fig. 34: Riggindale

Simply by studying the map, try to develop a mental image of what the landscape looks like. At first it isn't easy, but gradually it does all begin to make sense. The same is true of that of Figure 35, which shows the ground falling from High Street (behind the photographer) towards the saddle of the Straits of Riggindale.

Fig. 35: Descending to the Straits of Riggindale

It takes a good deal of practice to relate what you

see on the map to what you eventually see on the ground. Part of the initial problem is that the compression of the map over-exaggerates the narrowness of some features. Rough Crag, for example, looks frighteningly narrow in places, yet you can see from the picture that there's really plenty of room to walk. This is not always the case; ridges can become desperately narrow at times.

Now let's consider the second map (Figure 36), which shows a walk in the Chilterns.

First impressions:

- much gentler countryside, with contours widely spaced; but remember, because this is comparatively low-lying land, the contour interval is 5 metres not 10 metres

- considerably more woodland

- field boundaries

- roads

- some steep ground, especially facing north and west between Lodge, Coombe and Bacombe Hills.

Fig. 36: Extract from Explorer map 181 in the Chiltern Hills south-west of Wendover

A closer look shows:

- the woodland is a mix of pine and broadleaf

- the highest point is Coombe Hill, but that generally the land falls gently away to the east towards Wendover and more steeply northwards to the Vale of Aylesbury

- the Ridgeway National Trail follows the hill crests with the open summit of Coombe Hill a fabulous viewpoint (which is what the Fan-shaped blue symbol tells you).

Although you need a wider map extract to appreciate it fully, where the contours gather together to form a stretch of steep ground, as it does here below the Ridgeway, it actually makes what is known as an **escarpment** – a place where higher land, generally flatter, drops (or rises, depending on your point of view), and in effect creates an edge. Escarpments are common features of the British landscape and occur not only in the Chilterns, but in the Brecon Beacons of South Wales, in the Peak District, in North Yorkshire, even in Lancashire. Escarpments are excellent walking country, providing a lofty vantage point with good views over the surrounding countryside. Take a look at Figure 37, which shows a walker below the spectacular escarpment of the Cleveland Hills in North Yorkshire.

On the spur of the moment

Quite often the contours appear to go off in all directions, twisting this way and that, and it is not always easy to figure out where the valleys

Fig. 37: The Cleveland Hills escarpment

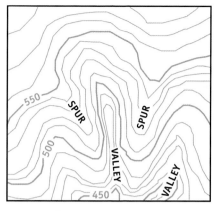

Fig. 38: Spurs and valleys

If the Vs or Us point uphill, it is a valley. If the Vs or Us point downhill, you're looking at a spur.

are. Of course, if there's a stream or a river shown, then that is a good clue, but in limestone country especially you might find large expanses with little evidence of watercourses, many of which disappear underground for part of their length.

Once again the clue to the solution lies in the contour heights shown on the map, remembering that the top of the number points uphill. If you now look at Figure 38, you can see that the contours of the valleys and the adjacent spurs have a rough V or U shape.

Planning a walk

It may be argued that it makes more sense at this point to take maps outside and begin the process of relating them to the landscape. But working out walks on a map is a continuing part of the process begun in the preceding chapter, that of learning to read what the map is telling you. And the ability to plan attractive walks is part of that development. For many it is as enjoyable as the walk itself. In fact, each year hardy backpackers set off alone or in small groups to walk from one side of Scotland to the other following no set route. They spend months planning their own route, tweaking it here and there, working out bad weather alternatives, reading the nuances of the map,

Planning is the key to a successful walk.

deciding where to camp or spend the night. The anticipatory pleasure in doing just that is considerable, and all the more so when you actually get out there, faithfully follow the route you planned, or making changes if the weather dictates that you should, and everything turns out fine.

A walk is not just the process of putting one foot in front of the other; it is everything from the detailed planning, weighing up the options, calculating distance and time, getting out there and doing it, and then coming home to a hot bath and a drop of whatever makes you feel good.

A walk is a package. Using *OS Maps* digital mapping makes the process easier and more reliable. So, it's useful to discuss both forms of mapping here, and to introduce *OS Maps*.

Introducing OS Maps

The *OS Maps* mobile app or online facility is a relatively new departure for Ordnance Survey, one that allows you to download OS leisure mapping to all of your mobile devices and in several formats. In addition to the customary mapping at 1:25000, 1:50000 and 1:250000 scales you can also see the mapping as an aerial view, 3D aerial or a 'standard' depiction, which gives a clearer presentation of the terrain.

With *OS Maps* on a screen in front of you (see Figure 39, and Figure 28, p44), it is possible to create a custom route – your intended walk – and for the software to calculate the distance and display a profile that gives the lowest and highest points along the route as well as the total ascent involved. You can also input your desired/likely walking speed, and the system will calculate an approximate time for the walk.

Once you're happy with your plotted route, you simply save it, print it out and carry it with you. The fact that your route is saved, also means that it will appear on your mobile device, together with your position along it, using its in-built GPS.

For good measure, *OS Maps* also gives you the current weather forecast for the destination of your walk both for the current day and for a further

Fig. 39: A route displayed in 3D Aerial in OS Maps; see Fig. 28 on p44 for the same route displayed over 1:25000 mapping

few days ahead. Moreover, the system shows the location of scheduled monuments, designated car parks, bus stops, places to stay, places to eat, including pubs, trig pillars and hills and mountains by category, e.g. Munros, Marilyns.

All of these factors can have a bearing on how you plan your walk.

What sort of walk are you planning?

There are many issues to consider when planning a walk, but they fall into two broad headings:

- Subjective: those where *you* make the decisions and the choices, and
- Objective: those over which you have no control.

Subjective aspects involve making decisions about:

- where you are intending to walk
- whether the walk is circular, out-and-back or linear – in the last case you will need to consider the transport logistics
- what distance you want to cover
- how much 'climbing' you want to include
- the extent to which you can keep the walk on footpaths rather than roads
- whether some footpaths more than others offer better views, take you through attractive villages, to popular beauty spots, or past pubs (or avoids these, if that is your preference)
- what 'escape routes' – see below – there are.

Objective considerations are:

- the weather – though you do have the choice of looking at the weather forecast and deciding to abort the walk if things look grim
- the terrain you will encounter – although you can go some way to assessing the type of terrain you will be crossing, when you finally get to grips with it you are invariably faced with aspects that just do not show on the map, e.g. knee-deep heather, land that is flooded after heavy rainfall, seasonal overgrowth, obstructions
- accidents – while everyone hopes that accidents will not happen, sadly they sometimes do, and the person planning the walk needs to know the quickest and safest route to safety from any stage of the walk
- changes in the weather – the day may start fine, but the British weather is unpredictable at best. The same 'escape route' planning that applies to potential accidents applies to the need to deal with sudden and unexpected adverse weather also.

There is another consideration, too. It is vitally important to devise a route that is not only within the physical ability of everyone involved, but also within the map reader's competence. Following field edges and country lanes in rural Oxfordshire is one thing, navigating across trackless moorland in the Western Highlands with the mist closing in is quite another. Fortunately the use of a GPS device comes to our aid here, and this is covered in a later chapter. But a GPS alone is no complete substitute for the raw ability to read and understand a map, and know your place on it.

The process of learning to map read and navigate is an incremental thing that adopts the walk-before-you-run philosophy. Take it, literally, one step at a time, and remember the word KISS – Keep It Stupidly Simple, or, if you prefer, Keep It Simple, Stupid!

The planning process

Once you have decided where you are going and have the relevant map, whether it's a paper map or a digital one, there are basically four stages in the planning process – see below. But it has to be said that at this stage you get a better idea of the lie of the land, and therefore your route across it, from studying a paper map opened fully in front of you rather than the more limited visual display you might get on a computer monitor or handheld device.

1. Identify the 'attractive' stretches you would like to include

Having understood what the information on the map is telling you, you start to get a feel for what the area you are intending to visit is like. Use a highlighter pen to pinpoint the appealing stretches, and if you particularly want to include a pub along the way then you will already have noticed that the Ordnance Survey *Explorer* maps do have a pub symbol. What the map doesn't tell you is what the beer or the food is like – there is only so much a map can do, after all.

2. Make connections

Look for the footpaths that connect the places you want to visit, noting any alternatives that may be possible, and gradually tease out a connection so that your route starts to take shape. Be prepared to revise your plans. The more you study the map, the more you see. You are trying to develop a walk that satisfies the aims you identified above, and with experience you acquire a feel for walks that meet your needs.

3. Is it good for you?

You next need to consciously assess the route against your aims.
• Is it the right length?

- Is the format what you wanted, e.g. circular or linear?
- Does it seem to be within the ability of those taking part?
- If it is a linear walk, what can you do about transport, e.g. is the finishing point on a bus route and will the buses be running? (A mobile signal and/or internet connectivity in rural areas cannot be relied upon, so detailed preparation before you begin a walk is imperative.)

4. Making adjustments

If the route is too long, find a way of reducing it – maybe start at a different point, or take a shortcut. If part of it looks too steep, find a way round that section. Keep repeating the process until you get the route you want.

TIP: There is one other little bit of planning you can do at this stage that has nothing to do with maps or route planning. Research. Do a little background research about the places you are visiting on the walk. This is a travel journalist's trick. There is nothing worse than spending a couple of hours exploring a castle, coming away and then discovering something even more fascinating tucked away in a nearby woodland.

How long will it take?

Does it matter? Well, yes, it does. And, no, it doesn't.

Imagine this: it's a lovely day, perfect for walking and everything is going exactly according to plan. Your map reading is spot on. You take a break by a stream and dangle your feet. Stop for coffee and a bite. There's a car and a change of clothing at the end of the walk. The sky is blue; the birds are singing.

Why do you want it to end? Does it matter how long the walk takes?

On the other hand: same scenario, except there isn't a car waiting. You have to catch a bus back to the start. It's the last bus. You can't afford to miss it.

Does it matter how long the walk takes? It does now; the consequences of missing that last bus may not be life threatening, but are you up to walking all the way back to the start in growing darkness?

Walking speed

The more walking you do, the better you become at roughly calculating how long the walk will take; you get to know your own abilities. So, on familiar terrain, 'distance' may be all you need to know to give you a fairly accurate idea of how much time to allow. Moreover, you get to know the length of walk that best suits you, whether it is 16 kilometres (10 miles) for a day-long walk, or 6 kilometres (3¾ miles) for an afternoon stroll.

Walking speed is a personal thing, geared not only to what you can physically achieve and can sustain for prolonged periods, but also to what you want to do. Walking is a recreation, not military training. Much as we might admire those super-fit military types who can romp across 80 kilometres (50 miles) and still have the energy for an hour in the gym, that is not what recreational walking is about. So, at one extreme you may find that, if you needed to, you could push on at 6 or 7km/hour (3¾–4 mph); at the other extreme you might be perfectly happy at 3km/hour (2 mph).

But that is far from true of everyone. Each of us has a comfortable walking speed; go beyond that and things start to become uncomfortable, leading to tiredness, sore feet and lowering of morale.

Of course, 'walking speed' assumes continuous progress, but makes no allowance for:

- voluntary stops, e.g. snack breaks, bird-watching, eating blackberries, calls of nature, 'other' distractions
- particularly difficult terrain
- pathless walking sections
- poor conditions underfoot, e.g. mud, ice, snow
- strong winds
- heavy loads
- unreliable knees.

Naismith's Rule

This simple rule has been in use for years; it is a good guide, but it is a worthwhile exercise to keep notes over a period of a few months and assess the time your walks actually take against Naismith's calculation. You may find that you are 10 per cent faster than Naismith, or 15 per cent slower. The value of this is that you can then always apply Naismith's Rule to your walks, and make this adjustment for your personal abilities.

The rule simply states that you allow one hour for each 5 kilometre (3 miles) of distance. Then add half an hour for each 300 metre (1,000 feet) of ascent (if you are planning your walk using a map with contours at 10 metre intervals, that conveniently breaks down to one minute for each contour line crossed).

Naismith's Rule applies only to those parts of the route that ascend; with descents it is assumed that they do not significantly affect your speed. But lengthy, steep descents, especially across poor ground, can really slow you down, and you need to add more time for this: around half of the time calculated for the ascents.

Of course, if your walk involves no significant ascents, then Naismith's Rule is needlessly rigorous. It is vital to know how long you think a walk should take, but a better idea evolves over a period of time of your own abilities: 16 kilometres (10 miles) on the flat = 'x' hours; 16 kilometres (10 miles) with a lot of ascent = 'y' hours.

Any problems?

The main problem with planning from a map is that you cannot be sure the footpaths are open, unobstructed and straightforward to follow. In some remote areas, paths may have fallen into disuse. In farming areas, fields may be ploughed over or full of cattle (including bulls); both may be a deterrent to progress, especially where there are livestock if you have a dog with you.

When planning a walk in an area that is new to you, mark up alternative routes in case you find your preferred route is in some way blocked.

Think ahead

When setting off on a walk it is a potentially life-saving practice to leave a note of your intended route and the time you think the walk will take with someone who can alert the emergency services if you fail to return reasonably close to your intended return time. Of course, this is not always possible, there may be no one you can leave a note with, and in any case this can fall foul of a number of seemingly irrelevant issues, like a decision to stop off at a pub, or to add some extra mileage, or the simple fact that it was a lovely day and you did not want the walk to end.

Using maps

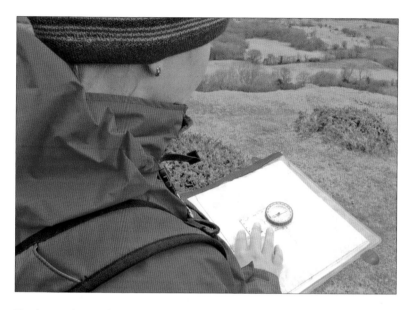

Having understood what a map is, and what all the marginal data means, it is now appropriate to begin the basic skills of navigation: how to use the map.

Setting the map

For the greater part of your walking you will constantly be relating the map in your hand to the ground you are walking, and vice versa. This is fundamental to navigation, it is ongoing, there is no end to it, and it's something you do all the time. In fact, you would be silly not to. And it applies equally to paper and digital maps.

'Setting the map' simply means holding the map so that the features on it roughly (ideally exactly) correspond with what you see in front of you, to the sides and even behind you.

Why is it important? Well, for a start, you need to take the correct route out of the car park.

There are two ways you can set the map. The first uses a compass (a gadget that will be more fully discussed in the next chapter); the other sets the map by the features around you.

Setting the map using a compass

To set the map using a compass, there are three steps (see Figure 40):

1. Set the N on the compass dial so that it aligns with the big arrow at the top of the compass.

2. Hold the compass on your map – near the edge is easier – so that the long edge of the compass is aligned with the grid lines on the map, and pointing north (not east!), i.e. to the top of the map.

3. Keep a tight hold of both map and compass, and, holding them horizontally, turn the whole map (and yourself) until the red end of the compass needle is aligned with the red arrow inside the circular dial.

Fig. 40: The three steps in setting the map

STEP 1
Set dial to north

STEP2
Align edge of compass with grid lines

STEP 3
Spin map and compass together to align needle with 'North' arrow in the dial

The map is now set, the top edge of the map is north, the left edge is west, the right, east, and the bottom, south, i.e. behind you. Now you can begin relating what you see in front of you, and all around you, with what you see on the map.

Try it with a few easy landmarks first, like a church steeple or the edge of a woodland or plantation. Of course, the moment you alter your position – if, for example, you spin through 90° – then the map needs to be reset. In fact, you could be resetting the map every time you change direction during a walk. But the more accomplished you become, the less is the need to do this. In any case, if you spend all your time looking at the map, you won't see anything of the countryside.

Setting a map by features

Using a compass to set a map is by far the most accurate way, but as you become more accomplished at using map and compass, so you can quickly learn to set the map simply by relating it to features that you see around you. Setting the map in this way means that you turn the map so that a feature you can see on the ground corresponds with the surrounding landscape in exactly the same relationship as on the map. Of course, it follows that setting a map by reference to features will only work when you can actually see identifiable features.

It is also true that to set a map by features, you need to know where you are in order to start identifying what is around you. But it works the other way, too – unless you are hopelessly lost. You can use that woodland over on the left, and that church with a tower directly ahead and the lake over on the right to give a rough idea of where you are. It isn't precise, but if the map is set, even at this degree of inaccuracy, you can at least stop yourself wandering off in the wrong direction – if you know your route lies between the church and the lake, and you find yourself heading for the woodland, something is wrong.

Finding your way

As you walk, map (or mobile) in hand, you should be constantly checking your position. You will find that you do keep track of your progress, but every so often you need to confirm exactly where you are, especially if a choice of routes lies ahead.

It is very reassuring (and confidence-building) to realise just how frequently you get the map reading right. As a 'novice' navigator, you should check the map every time you make a major change of direction, but then less frequently, as you become more experienced.

In time you are almost subconsciously **ticking off** what might be called 'reassurance points': field boundary junctions, farms, rivers and streams – even the most able navigators do this, regularly. It will (should) be something you do every time you go for a walk. But what if some of the features you are looking for are missing? There will be one of three possible reasons:

- You are not at the position you pinpointed, i.e. temporarily lost.
- You made a mistake in plotting the position during the planning stage.
- You are at the pinpoint position, but what you're looking for has been removed. This could be a field boundary, but it could also be something much larger, like a building that has been demolished. It takes a long time for changes like this to find their way onto mapping.

If you are in the correct position, then there will often be enough other features nearby to help you to position yourself. Often the best navigational aids are there in front of you – walls and fences, and, more to the point, the way they bend or suddenly change direction, and, of course, the path itself, waymarks and signposts. You can find totally barren and signpostless landscapes if you try hard enough. But mostly, it isn't like that.

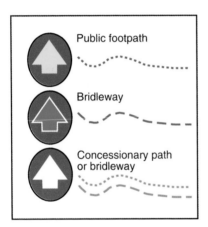

Fig. 41: Conventional waymarks and corresponding map depiction for footpaths and bridleways

Routes across farmland are often waymarked, and the type of waymark links in with the three principal routes as depicted on maps. Figure 41 shows the map delineation from Ordnance Survey *Explorer* maps.

Signposts also abound, and are usually found at major changes of route direction, and track or path junctions (see Figure 42). Stand beside a signpost at a known path junction, and, as with a trig pillar, you know exactly where you are.

Walking with paper and digital maps

Digital mapping for public consumption is New Age. There is a learning curve, but it isn't particularly steep, and everything you need to know, certainly if you're using *OS Maps*, is just a click away – you can even get to view a fly-through of your walk, and see the route from an aerial perspective.

The arguments against resorting to digital devices in an outdoors

Fig. 42: Without this signpost on Sleights Moor in the North York Moors, Coast-to-Coast walkers may well miss the turning

setting are well known: poor/diminishing battery life, getting/losing a signal, what if it gets wet, or you drop it and it breaks, or you lose it? With paper maps you don't have to worry about batteries, signals or the map malfunctioning. Moreover, these days you can get waterproof mapping, so that deals with the rain. So, that seems to lean in favour of paper mapping.

When walking with a map, always rotate the map so that the route you are following is going away from you. This way, you will not mix up 'lefts' and 'rights'.

But the short answer is, use both. A digital map will show you where you are along your route, whether you're deviating from it; a paper map can't do that. Equally, digital maps, confined as they are to a small screen, whether *OS Maps* or other digital devices, don't show you the bigger picture in the way that an opened paper map does. But paper maps blow about in the wind, digital maps don't... and so it goes on.

Compass

There is nothing mystical about a compass. At its basic level, a compass consists of a magnetised pointer free to align itself accurately with the Earth's magnetic field. The Chinese are credited with 'inventing' the compass in the year 271, one of the four great inventions of ancient China, although there are references in Chinese literature to magnetism 2,500 years ago.

Modern hand-held compasses use a magnetised needle or dial inside a fluid-filled capsule; the fluid causes the needle to 'dampen' rather than oscillate back and forth around magnetic north.

Most modern recreational compasses integrate a protractor with the compass, using a separate magnetised needle. In this design the rotating housing containing the magnetised needle is fitted with orienting lines and an orienting arrow, and then mounted in a transparent base plate containing a direction-of-travel (DOT) indicator for use in taking bearings directly from a map.

Other features can include romer scales for measuring distances and plotting positions on maps, luminous markings or bezels for use at night or in poor light, and various sighting mechanisms for taking bearings of distant objects with greater precision.

But surely all you need to know is which way is 'North'? This is true, but if a compass can help in other ways, then so much the better.

The first rules of navigation

There are four basic rules to begin with:

Rule 1: Buy a compass.
Rule 2: Learn how to use it.
Rule 3: Always have it with you when out walking.
Rule 4: Trust it.

There is nothing difficult about reading and using a compass, so do not persuade yourself otherwise. Let's start by looking at the basics of the compass – see Figure 43.

Scale: In this illustration, the scale is in centimetres, but it could equally be in millimetres. This sort of scale ruler is useful in calculating distance against a map. To do that, you need to know that with 1:25000 maps, 4 centimetres equals 1 kilometre; on 1:50000 maps, 2 centimetres equals 1 kilometre. NOTE: The particular compass used in this illustration also has a romer down each side, one at a scale of 1:25000 and the other at 1:50000 which, in this respect, make the scale along the top less vital. But not all compasses have romers. If your compass does not have a romer, you might consider buying one that does; it saves you having to remember whether it is 2 or 4 centimetres that equal 1 kilometre.

Fig. 43: Basic compass

Scale

Direction-of-travel (DOT) arrow

1:25000 romer

Base plate

Magnifying lens

1:50000 romer

Housing arrow and orienting lines

Needle (red end points to magnetic north)

Magnifying glass: You may take the view that there is nothing wrong with your eyesight, but for most of us that will not always be the case. That little circular lens helps with the fine detail of maps, especially to show the way through farmyards, for example, or which side of a field boundary a path follows. A magnifying lens is not essential, but if you are buying a new compass, then buy one with a lens.

Base plate: Nothing magical here; that's all it is, a base plate.

Housing arrow and orienting lines: This is the compass housing. Inside it sits the compass needle. The housing, which rotates easily, is filled with a liquid which 'dampens' the needle's movement, otherwise the needle would swing to and fro for ages.

Sometimes, mainly because of changes in atmospheric pressure caused by being at higher altitude, a bubble will develop in the liquid. If the bubble is small and has no effect on the swing of the needle, you can continue to use the compass. But if the bubble is large, you need a new compass. It's like a waterproof watch: once you get water in there, you cannot get it out – it's the same with compass bubbles, which remain stubbornly in the housing even when you go back to lower altitudes.

Underneath the needle are the orienting lines, the lines that allow you to line up the compass housing with grid lines on a map. The two central lines are drawn as an arrow. This is the housing arrow, and it points to wherever you turn the housing to point to, although it is a good idea always to return it to north. Around the edge of the housing are the cardinal points of the compass – North, South, East and West – and smaller sub-divisions of 2°, marked up at 20° intervals.

Needle: Typically red (and sometimes also luminous) at the north end and black or white at the other.

Direction-of-travel (DOT) arrow: The DOT arrow runs through the magnifying lens from the edge of the compass housing. This is the bit of the compass that will point you in the direction you need to take.

Types of compass

There are various types of compass, and you get what you pay for. If you want to, you can buy a sighting compass like that shown in Figure 44.

But before you invest in one of the more sophisticated compasses that are available on the market, it makes sense to start with something uncluttered and uncomplicated like a basic expedition compass – see Figure 45.

Or just a simple field compass – see Figure 46 – is perfectly adequate.

A small point

If you look closely at Figure 43 on page 69, you'll see that within the housing arrow the letters 'MN' (for Magnetic North) appear. If you never intend to take your compass beyond the northern hemisphere, then you can forget these letters, because they simply tell you that the compass is for use in the northern hemisphere.

If you are going to a destination outside the northern hemisphere and need a compass, buy a new one when you reach your destination.

Fig. 44: A 'sighting' compass

How attractive are you?

Because a compass relies on magnetism, many things, including your own personal magnetism, can affect the way the compass works. The usual culprits are cameras around your neck, mobile phone in your breast pocket, metal zips, and even the underwiring in a bra, or even a pacemaker, if you happen to need one.

Before you set off on a walk, test the compass by holding it in various positions to see whether anything is affecting the way the needle swings. If the needle is affected, you may need to make adjustments – move the phone to another pocket, for example – or simply hold the compass away from your body.

Fig. 45: An 'expedition' compass

Magnetic rocks

Having now digested everything you need to know about

Fig. 46: A 'field' compass

compasses, there is one more snippet of information that will make all that learning quite useless: magnetic rocks.

In some areas of the UK, notably among the Cuillin on the Isle of Skye, but in other places, too, there are rock types that are high in iron content, and these will affect your compass reading, especially if the magnetic field is particularly strong locally.

Opinions differ about the extent to which this sort of influence affects compass readings. But, when the iron-bearing rocks were lain down as molten lava, millions of years ago, magnetic north was in quite a different location than where you find it now, and it is that old magnetic north that is locked into the rocks, and will deflect compass readings.

The Cuillin on the Isle of Skye

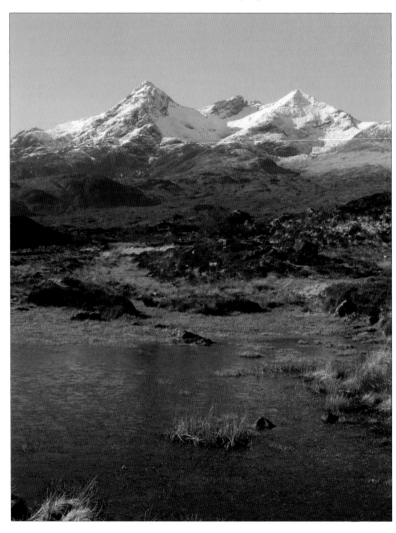

Using compasses

Wonderful as compasses are, experienced navigators always make the point that they are no substitute for good map reading skills, merely an additional prop. Good navigators are always checking the route for mapped features as they walk, using these to fix their position as an ongoing process. The skill in practical map reading is not to walk for a while and then ask, 'Where are we?', but to be constantly checking.

What the compass does is to show remarkably accurate direction on the ground, i.e. the direction of your route, or a distant feature. While there is an abundance of mapped features around you, following a route using just the map is comparatively easy. Where a compass comes into its own is when mapped features are few and far between, or, at the other extreme, there are so many features that they become confusing, making it difficult to decide on the route clearly.

Although a compass is fundamentally a simple device, using it in the early stages of learning navigational skills can be a little daunting and baffling. So, we need to KISS (Keep It Stupidly Simple, remember?). Thankfully, it does not take long to get the hang of it, but regular practice will soon reap its rewards.

The main use for a compass is to tell you which way to go, whenever there is doubt, or as a reassurance factor – just checking. But a compass alone cannot do this. What is needed is to take a **bearing**.

What is a bearing?

A bearing is simply the angle between 'North', where you are and where you want to go. Bearings are defined by expressing the number of degrees (expressed as x°) between 0° and 360° in a clockwise direction from North to the direction of travel. Look at Figure 47.

A bearing is the angle 'x': the angle between 'N', 'A' and 'C' – in this case 40°. So, Point C lies on a bearing of 40° from your present position. 'C' might be a distant feature, or simply

Fig. 47: A bearing

N
North

C
Target

x°

A
You

the continuation of a path you are following which is momentarily out of sight over the brow of a domed field. Equally it may be nothing more complicated than confirming which of a number of paths that converge at your location is the correct one to take.

Taking a bearing on the map

What you now need to do is to figure out the bearing (A–C) on the map from your known position to your target destination.

There are three steps in taking a bearing:

Step 1: Place your compass on the map so that one of the long edges joins both the point where you are and your destination point (or direction, if it is simply a path), making sure that the DOT arrow is pointing towards (or along) your target.

Step 2: Rotate the compass housing so that the housing arrow is parallel with the N–S grid lines on the map – see Figure 48. Make sure that in both these steps you are as accurate as possible; cutting down on error now will reduce the risk of difficulty later.

> *When calculating a bearing, do a rough estimate first. It does not need to be accurate, between 0° and 90° will suffice. Once you have taken the bearing, if it roughly compares with your 'guesstimate', that is fine; if not, something is wrong.*

Step 3: Read off the bearing on the compass housing next to the direction-of-travel arrow – see Figure 48.

Some simple mistakes

Everyone makes a few simple mistakes when learning how to use a compass. The main thing is to do the learning in a safe location, not standing in the middle of wild moorland.

Mistake 1: The compass is not aligned in the direction-of-travel – A to C in Figure 47. If your compass is aligned C to A, you will get a reading that is incorrect by 180°.

Mistake 2: The orienting lines in the compass housing are not aligned to the north of the map. An error of 180° will result again, if you do this the wrong way round.

Align grid lines and the orienting line in the compass housing

Read bearing here

Ignore the compass needle at this stage

Fig. 48: Use your compass as a protractor to measure the bearing

---

The importance of accuracy

When working with map and compass it is important to be as accurate as possible – make sure locations are very precisely lined up. Fail to do this and errors will creep in.

But how much of a problem is it? If you are simply trying to determine whether the path in front of you heads off in the right direction, then it's not much of a problem at all.

If you are deciding between two paths that are fairly close together, it could be more critical, but probably not life threatening.

But if a wall junction to where your route continues is a kilometre distant over the brow of a hill, you need to be sure of your direction.

Or if you are trying to decide between two narrow, descending ridges in poor visibility, then failing to be accurate could result in very serious consequences.

Magnetic variation revisited

'Understanding North' touched briefly on magnetic variation. It is now time to take a closer look.

Magnetic variation is the difference between grid north and magnetic north (see Figure 49).

Grid north is at the top of your map; magnetic north is wandering about the frozen wastes of the Arctic Ocean, slowly moving east.

Moreover, the direction of magnetic north varies depending on where you are. It varies across the UK and in 2014, for the first time in 350 years, in Cornwall, Pembrokeshire and in parts of the Outer Hebrides, magnetic north moved to the east of grid north. This change is anticipated to sweep gradually eastwards, crossing the UK by 2030. In March 2019, the magnetic variation at Plymouth was 0°13' east of grid north, and in Norwich it was 2°29' west of grid north. Magnetic variation is indicated in the marginal data on maps. Ordnance Survey *Explorer* 296 states: *Magnetic north is estimated at 0°30' west of grid north for July 2020* (see Figure 3, p13). Annual change is approximately 12' (12 minutes, or 0.2°) east. As Ordnance Survey maps are produced at different intervals, and relate to different parts of the country, you will find that information about magnetic variation is different on each map.

Fig. 49: Magnetic variation

Diagrammatic only

If you want to know the magnetic variation for any part of the country then you can visit the website for the British Geological Society where there is a magnetic variation calculator (http://www.geomag.bgs.ac.uk).

For demonstration purposes in this book through pages 76-80, magnetic variation is taken to be 4° west.

Is that far? And does it matter? You can do the mathematics if you wish, but the fact is that over a distance of a kilometre, a 4° error will put you 70 metres off course. Close enough, in good visibility and a safe location, but how would you feel about being 70 metres adrift in thick mist on a windswept moor or a mountain ridge? Add to this the fact that most compasses are made to be accurate to a tolerance of ± 4°, and you could be 140 metres out. How critical is that?

Walking with map and compass

Now that you understand how to take bearings, it is time to go out so that you can start putting what you've learned into practice.

First, we have calculated what magnetic variation is, but what do we do with it?

Need we bother with magnetic variation at all?

We saw in the last chapter that a 4° variation will have a 70 metres deviation over a distance of 1 kilometre. It therefore follows that as the distance, i.e. the 1 kilometre, gets less, so the 'error' is less. And if all you are doing is checking which of two paths a few strides in front of you is the correct one to follow, you can safely ignore magnetic variation altogether. You can also ignore it when setting the map (see 'Using maps', p63). But conversely the greater the distance you need to travel on a bearing, the greater the risk of error, and the greater the need to allow for magnetic variation.

One solution would be to ensure that each 'leg' on which you are using a bearing is shorter rather than longer. Of course this may not always be possible because at the end of each leg you need to be somewhere that you can accurately identify on the map, e.g. a field boundary corner. But if there is nothing at all, you have no choice but to navigate over a longer distance. In this circumstance, magnetic variation does play a role, and the need to be very accurate comes into play.

How to allow for magnetic variation

When you take a bearing using your compass and the map, i.e. you have taken a bearing from your known position to a distant point, then the bearing you have taken is called a grid bearing, because it is taken from the grid on the map. Now you need to allow for magnetic variation.

The same is true if you are not entirely sure of your position, and want to use your compass to take a bearing of a distant feature, e.g. a building, and then want to use it to trace your position. This bearing, because you took it without reference to the map, i.e. just using magnetism, is called a magnetic bearing, a topic that will be returned to shortly.

Many people, and not just those who are learning the skills of map and compass work, find it confusing to remember what to do about magnetic variation. Clearly, if you think about it, if you take a bearing on a map, it will not be the same bearing as the one you take – assuming you can see your target – just using the compass. So, there is a little saying to remember whether to add or subtract that 4° (but in reality, the value given in the legend of the OS map for the area you're walking in, or the British Geological Society figure for your approximate location) of magnetic variation, and it works:

| Men Generally Say | M-G-S | Magnetic to Grid Subtract |
| Great Minds Agree | G-M-A | Grid to Magnetic Add |

So, if you have taken a bearing on a map (grid bearing), say 40°, then to convert to a compass bearing you need to add magnetic variation (4°), to give 44°. And that is the compass bearing you now walk along.

There is another way that will be discussed shortly, but for now we need to know how to walk with a compass on a bearing.

Walking on a bearing
You have taken a bearing on a map of, say, 65°. You have added 4° to allow for magnetic variation to give 69° - see Figure 50. (NOTE: if magnetic variation is east of grid north rather than west of it, then you should subtract magnetic variation not add it.)

Hold the compass, as level as possible (as shown in Figure 51).

Now, without touching the compass housing, and holding the compass level, spin your entire body round until the compass needle lines up with the north arrow (red on red) – Figure 52.

Fig. 50: The compass is set on your grid bearing 65°, and magnetic variation (4°) has been added

Fig. 51: Hold the compass level, slightly away from your body, to allow for 'personal' magnetism, but not too far. Keep your elbows tucked in

When you have done this, the direction-of-travel arrow will now point the way to walk. (So, off you go.)

That alternative technique for coping with magnetic variation mentioned earlier is one orienteers use. Instead of worrying about whether to add or subtract magnetic variation, they set the compass to the grid bearing (65° in this example), and simply point the compass needle to 4° west instead of north. The effect is the same.

Is it that easy?

If all you wanted the bearing for was to choose between two or more footpaths a short distance in front of you, then, yes, it is that easy.

Fig. 52: The compass is now aligned to north (red on red)

But if you took the bearing because your target was out of sight over the brow of a hill, then you need some intermediate reference point to be sure you are taking the right line. This reference point needs to be something you can positively identify, and which will not move (so not a sheep).

See Figure 53 – the direction-of-travel lies across this heather moor, and the distant mound can be used as an intermediate objective. If the mound is also shown on the map – in this case it is a known tumulus – then that is a bonus because you can recalculate your direction once you get to the

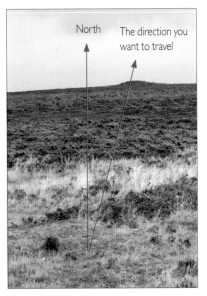

Fig. 53: Look for a 'target' along the direction you want to travel

mound. But quite often the terrain is not so accommodating, and you must continue to walk along your bearing, looking for new intermediate reference points as you go.

The important thing is that the intermediate reference point is on your bearing, and not off to one side. Experienced navigators can learn to cope with things not being perfectly aligned, but it is a 'no-go zone' for anyone less practised. This process of 'looking ahead' is a vital part of skilful navigation. Not only is it important, as here, with actual navigation, but it is a key part of the state of total awareness that is essential to successful walking.

Once you have identified an intermediate reference point, put your compass away, taking care not to disturb its setting (or make a note of your bearing, just in case), and then walk to your objective. On rough ground

Trust your compass, not your intuition.

it is important to see where you are putting your feet, while on a smooth, grassy hillside you want to enjoy the walk. When you get to the intermediate objective, take out the compass and repeat the whole process until you get to where you are going.

While navigating in this way across fairly easy terrain in good conditions, things are straightforward. But poor visibility and tiredness can disorientate you and persuade you that the compass is somehow giving a wrong reading. If you have done everything correctly, do not be tempted to over-ride your compass; it never gets tired, doesn't have batteries that can die, and always points to north.

Taking a back bearing

To develop confidence in what you are doing, it is useful to use a back bearing to check on your progress. Taking back bearings, however, assumes that you can still see where you started your current leg of the journey from – if you cannot, you are on your own. But, if your start point is still visible, then, without altering anything on the compass, simply spin round so that the white end of the needle points to the red housing arrow (white on red). The direction-of-travel arrow will now point back the way you came.

Can anything go wrong?

There are five steps to ensuring that there is nothing wrong with your technique:

1. Position your compass edge precisely between where you are and where you want to go.

2. Ensure the direction-of-travel arrow points in the right direction when you are doing Step 1.

3. Take care to avoid pointing the housing arrow to the bottom of the map – the housing arrow points north, to the top of the map.

4. Make proper allowance for magnetic variation.

5. Ensure the compass orienting lines are exactly parallel with the map grid lines.

Summary

1. *Place the edge of the compass on your map so that it joins where you are and where you want to go.*

2. *Ensure that the direction-of-travel arrow is pointing in the direction you want to go.*

3. *Turn the compass housing so that the orienting lines are parallel with the vertical grid lines on the map.*

4. *Read the bearing against the direction-of-travel arrow and add the magnetic variation shown in the map's marginal data.*

[NOTE: If magnetic variation is east of grid north rather than west of it, then you would subtract magnetic variation not add it.]

5. *Spin yourself bodily around so that the red end of the compass needle lines up with the red housing arrow.*

6. *The direction-of-travel arrow now points the way to go.*

7. *Look along your direction-of-travel and identify a feature along the bearing that you can safely walk to.*

Some basic techniques

The skills of advanced navigation all derive from the basics contained in this book. But it is important to ensure that these basics are fully understood before venturing into the sort of terrain (and conditions) where more sophisticated techniques are needed. The fundamentals of map reading and basic navigation must become second nature. But there is no mystery to advanced navigation, just the importance of getting the basics right first.

So, this chapter offers a few additional techniques that will be useful. None of what follows is an exact science, and much of it varies from person to person.

Estimating distance on the ground

Experienced golfers can calculate distances to the green on a golf course with incredible accuracy. But for most people, the ability to estimate distance is not easy. Anyone who ever ran 100 metres at school, can make a fair stab at visualising the track distance on any terrain. But with greater distances, being able to look out across a landscape and estimate how far it is to a particular feature is difficult. Nor can it be taught; only practice makes perfect.

Pacing

Imagine that you are on some moorland track from which your intended route diverts after 250 metres. You need to be sure when you have travelled that distance, and 'pacing' is a way of getting it remarkably accurate. But everyone's pace length is different, and everyone's pace is affected by varying terrain. So, you have to begin by seeing how many double paces you personally take for a given distance.

Find a level stretch of ground near home, and see how many double paces, i.e. left foot (or right foot) hitting the ground, you take to cover, say, 100 metres. Test it a few times, to arrive at an average. For most people of average height it will be around 65, but people come in different shapes and sizes, so working out your own stride pattern is important if this technique is to be used. If you have a partner with whom you intend to walk, then get them to check their pacing as well, so that when you are out on the hill both of you can do the pacing. Four legs are better than two.

As an example, if you need to leave a path after 250 metres, you now know that you have to take 65 + 65 + 32½ double paces. That will put you there or thereabouts. But your stride pattern will be affected by slopes, difficult terrain, especially deep heather, and even fatigue, so you will need to make allowance for this.

Dealing with obstacles

Pacing comes into its own on boggy moorland, when your intended route may be barred by a small lake or expanse of boggy ground. If you can see where you are heading this is not so much of a problem, but if you are walking on a bearing you need to know how to negotiate the obstacle, and get back on course.

Fig. 54: Pacing around an obstacle

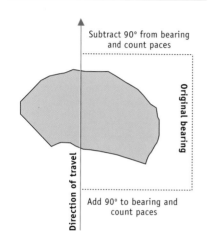

Subtract 90° from bearing and count paces

Original bearing

Direction of travel

Add 90° to bearing and count paces

Look at Figure 54. You are walking on a bearing and encounter an obstacle, in this case a small lake or pond. It is important that you do not lose your original bearing, and that you get back exactly on course.

To negotiate the lake, add exactly 90° to your bearing, and walk along this, counting your paces as you go, until you are clear of the end of the obstacle. Now revert to your original bearing, and walk until you are beyond the other side of the lake. Then subtract 90° from your original bearing, and walk along this, counting the paces until you equal the number of paces used in the first diversion. Finally, revert to your original bearing and resume the walk.

Aiming off

The practice of 'aiming off' is a good one and, a useful tool. Look at Figure 55. You are walking from Point A to Point B. Visibility is poor, and the chance of missing Point B on this stretch of moorland is significant. Only a small error to the left (north) could have you missing the wall altogether. The technique of aiming off avoids the error. Put simply, you take your bearing from Point A to Point B, and then just walk to the right, i.e. south, of it – in this illustration, towards Point C. Here there is a field boundary – a wall, in fact – and once you reach it, all you have to do is turn left and walk beside the wall until you reach Point B,

Fig. 55: Aiming off

immediately to the north of a wall junction.

The feature towards which you aim off need not be a wall, of course. It could equally be a stream, river, or the edge of woodland. If you try to hit Point B directly, and miss, you have no way of knowing whether you need to walk left or right to find it. Aiming off ensures that you find your target.

GPS

Although new technology continues to hit the market at bewildering speed, GPS (Global Positioning System) is here to stay, and has a useful role to play for walkers. It is vital to understand, however, that a GPS device, i.e. something that makes use of the GPS system, is not a substitute for map and compass skills; you need to understand everything that has preceded this chapter before you can use a GPS efficiently.

What is GPS?

GPS is a US-based worldwide radio navigation system that uses a network of 32 satellites and receivers to calculate positions. When using a GPS device, the known variable is where the satellites are, not where you are. The satellites essentially use known time (atomic clock) and location

> *Walkers should not rely on GPS as their only means of navigation; think of it as complementary to your map and compass, not as a substitute.*

which is transmitted to a receiver. By measuring the time a signal takes to reach the receiver, the distance from the satellite can be estimated. Repeat this with several satellites and the receiver can then use triangulation to establish its position.

There are alternative systems to GPS:

GLONASS, or 'Global Navigation Satellite System', is a Russian space-based satellite navigation system operating as part of a radio navigation satellite service.

GALILEO is similar to GPS, but owned and operated by the European Union and European Space Agency. It was developed to avoid the need to rely on the US (GPS) and Russian (GLONASS) systems.

In terms of positional accuracy GPS is slightly better than GLONASS overall, but due to the different positioning of the GLONASS satellites, GLONASS has better accuracy at high latitudes (far north or south). Most high-end GPS devices will automatically connect both to GPS and GLONASS, or give you the option of doing so.

The receivers used by walkers are hand-held devices that have a small aerial that picks up the signals. Using geometry, the receiver can work out where you are and, if it can connect with enough satellites, it can also work out your altitude. For the system to work, however, it follows that your hand-held device must have a clear view of the sky. Generally this is not a problem, but prolonged periods in dense woodland, for example, can cause the signal to drop.

The types of GPS devices available today are several in number,

Fig. 56: Examples of GPS devices

ranging from a smart phone, even a watch and tablets of various sizes, up to a dedicated GPS device such as those made by Garmin, SatMap or the OS Trail GPS.

The smallest of these, a watch, has obvious viewing limitations, since the screen, such as it is, will be very small. Smart phones are more useful, and the author regularly uses one for geocaching purposes. But for route navigation over prolonged distances, there is no substitute for something like the SatMap type of device, a Garmin or OS Trail (see Figure 56) with in-built mapping on which your position is constantly overlain.

Of course, when it comes to using high-end devices, they come with high-end prices. But if such a device gets you out of difficulty, or even saves your life, isn't it worth it?

> *Your location is the most valuable piece of information your GPS provides, and this alone is sufficient reason for having one.*

Information that a GPS device can provide

The information that a GPS provides can be presented in different ways because you determine the units of measurement you prefer – grid references, latitude and longitude, metres, feet, etc.

Fundamentally, a GPS tells you where you are. It can also give you your current altitude (although this particular reading can be erratic for several reasons, and should not be critically relied on). It will also record information about the route you are walking, in the form of a track log, and this is useful for a couple of reasons:

1. If you need to backtrack to your starting point, you can put the GPS 'in reverse', using its trackback function, and it will guide you back the way you came.

2. Saving your track log at the end of a walk on your device allows it to be exported (GPX file format) and uploaded to *OS Maps* (see page 44), or other bespoke mapping software programs, so that it overlays OS *Explorer* mapping to give a reasonably accurate depiction of your route.

The facility to pre-store a planned route is useful, enabling you to use the GPS to guide you along a route. Of course, the GPS does not know the condition of the terrain and it may link two waypoints by a route it is impossible to follow. So, this aspect of the GPS system needs treating with a measure of caution.

At any stage in a walk, you can 'mark', i.e. save, your position, and the GPS will store this. If, later, you need to return to any particular position, the GPS will guide you to it.

Understanding the limitations of GPS

Notwithstanding the versatility of a GPS device, it is important to look on it as complementary to a map and compass, not as a substitute. For this reason, you are advised always to carry the relevant maps and a compass. If you are using map and compass alone you need to set the map and figure out where you are on it. In cold, wet and windy weather this can be irksome, if not impossible. And because a GPS device containing maps gives you this information instantly, it is tempting to rely on the GPS. This is understandable, but not advised. In any case, it

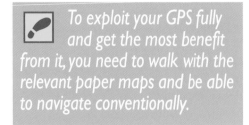

To exploit your GPS fully and get the most benefit from it, you need to walk with the relevant paper maps and be able to navigate conventionally.

does no harm to open up a map and take a look at the bigger picture of the landscape around you from time to time.

Accuracy

Accuracy depends on the number of satellites the receiver can 'see' and the signal strength. But experience has shown that the best accuracy the receiver itself will admit to is around +/- 3 metres. This, for walking purposes, is good enough in all but the most critical situations, e.g. on a knife-edge ridge.

The accuracy of a GPS device can be affected by a number of things, from tree cover to surrounding buildings, walking through underpasses and in tunnels, the position of your own body and even the atmosphere, which is the single most significant cause of signal error. But the state of the weather itself as a rule does not affect your GPS readings.

Any other problems?

There are a couple of issues.

- The first is that the hand-held device is battery operated, and even with long-life batteries, it will run out at some stage. So you have to carry spare batteries in your rucksack, and be attentive to the battery condition of your receiver at all times. If weight isn't an issue, you could always carry a power bank (fully charged, obviously), or one of those solar power banks that charges itself from sunlight (hopefully).

- The second point has already been touched on: your device needs to be able to 'see' the satellites, but woodland, high cliffs or overhanging rock, and tall buildings might all prevent this. Once a GPS loses its signal it can no longer track and record your route. When you 'reappear' it continues, but the trail displayed

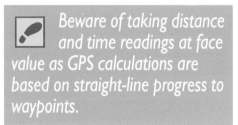

Beware of taking distance and time readings at face value as GPS calculations are based on straight-line progress to waypoints.

on the hand-held receiver has breaks in it, and if you download the track to a computer then the route for this blind stretch is shown as a straight line joining the last and next known readings.

- Hand-held receivers work best when held horizontally, and will not update until you physically move. It is possible to store a receiver in a jacket pocket and for it to successfully record a route, but better results are obtained if it is held externally.

- There is a danger of placing too much reliance on readings relating to forecasts of time and distance. Your GPS device will connect points by a straight line, and calculate time and distance accordingly. But it is rarely the case out in the countryside that we travel in a straight line, even before we called in the pub!

Initialising your GPS

Because GPS devices come in several 'brands', shapes and sizes, no specific guidance to any one device will be given here. Familiarising yourself with your GPS device will take time; not all of them are intuitive. But it only needs to be done once.

The first stage is to initialise your device, i.e. in effect to get it turned on and functioning. This is not something you can do indoors. You need to be out in the open, with a clear view of the sky (and not just upwards – most satellites lie to the south when viewed from the northern hemisphere).

In order for GPS receivers to function, they need to know three critical pieces of information. These are:

1. the current date and time
2. the receiver's location on the Earth's surface, and
3. the location of the satellites in orbit, known as 'ephemeris' data

When a GPS device has these three pieces of information, it performs a normal start-up procedure, called a 'warm start', and will typically begin displaying a position in less than one minute. But when a GPS device does not have this information, it must carry out a much slower 'cold start', which could take up to 20 minutes. Your very first use of a device will be a cold start, so be patient. After that, provided you remain more or less in the same neck of the woods, your device will 'remember' where to look in the sky to acquire a signal. But if you live in, say, the south of England, and take a holiday in the north of Scotland, things have changed, and your device will need a bit more time to figure things out.

Most GPS receivers have a satellite status screen that displays while the receiver is 'acquiring' satellites – see Figure 57, top image.

Once you have successfully initialised your GPS device, you will need to make some adjustments to meet your preferences. Again these only need to be done once, and include:

- Time format – 24-hour, 12-hour

- The layout of the 'Display' page, i.e. the page you see when using the device

- The position format, i.e. whether you use the grid system (preferable for walking) or co-ordinates based on latitude and longitude

- The Map datum – the default setting on your GPS device will be WGS84 (World Geodetic System 1984). This may change if you use your device in another country, but most devices have a list of the commonly used datums

- Units of measurement – set them as you wish: miles, kilometres, feet, metres, etc.

You will also need to set up the compass within the device to ensure that it points where you want it to, i.e. magnetic north. Different devices give differing instructions for doing this, but the method basically consists of opening the 'Compass' page, holding the device level, then spinning slowly round while you hold the device for a few moments to allow it to locate magnetic north. It will display a message once the compass is set to let you know that you can stop spinning.

Fig. 57: Screens on the Garmin eTrex10: Satellite, Compass, Trip Computer and Menu

Set your GPS to magnetic north if you want to use it in conjunction with your compass.

Walking with map and GPS

If your device does not have mapping built in or added via an SD card, then it is essential that you carry paper mapping, and refer to it in the same way that you would using the map and compass techniques described in an earlier chapter. In essence, all you are doing is using the GPS as a compass to demonstrate and confirm your direction of travel. You will certainly get more out of your GPS device if you use it in conjunction with paper mapping.

Many of the high-end GPS devices come with in-built mapping. Some mapping may be at a scale of 1:25000, some at 1:50000. Some devices have the mapping for a particular region supplied on an SD card, and most of these have a facility to toggle between the map scales. In fact, on some devices you can enlarge the scale considerably more, allowing you to see more clearly whether a path goes one side or the other of a boundary wall, for example.

The trouble with waypoints

Some guidebooks, such as the Pathfinder® Guides, provide a limited list of GPS waypoints, which can be pre-loaded into your device, and called up as your walk progresses. But do keep in mind that these waypoints will be connected by your GPS device in a straight line, which may not be one you can safely, or sensibly, walk. In this kind of guide, the waypoints are not there for you to navigate by, for the above reason. But they are helpful in letting you know when you have arrived at a critical point in the walk, such as a road or track junction, or a point of deviation from one pathway onto a diverging one.

Being able to follow a route, whether one that uses downloaded waypoints, or one you worked out at home before setting off, and see your position pinpointed on a map on your GPS device is very re-assuring. You have only to think about what it would be like if you were confronted with white-out conditions on a remote hillside. Knowing exactly where you are could well be a matter of life or death.

Geocaching

Introduced in 2000, geocaching is a cross between treasure hunting and orienteering, an adjunct to recreational walking that adds a new dimension to a visit to the countryside. It is a classic example of the combination of mapping and a GPS device since it is possible to download a geocaching app to a smart phone and use it in the same way you can use *OS Maps* (see below).

The pursuit is one that can be enjoyed by all, young and old alike, singly or in groups.

Tree cover might impact on the strength of a satellite signal

GPS and OS maps

Mention has been made in an earlier chapter about the system of digital mapping now available for a nominal annual subscription from Ordnance Survey – *OS Maps*. Its many attributes are detailed earlier. But the beauty of this system is that you can access the mapping on all your devices, GPS, smart phone (see Figure 58), iPad/tablet, etc. Until *OS Maps* came on the scene, using digital mapping for navigational purposes required the use either of ancillary software programs or mapping applications supplied on memory cards. With *OS Maps*, the two combine.

In terms of devising a route, all that's required is to open *OS Maps*, preferably on a desktop or laptop computer, search for a location close to where you intend to walk,

Fig. 58: OS Maps app on a mobile phone

and adjust the map so that your walk area is centred. Now, simply draw your intended route on the map using the 'Plot' tool.

Remembering the potential problems with waypoints, it follows that the more waypoints you create on a walk route the less the likelihood of encountering navigational difficulties. This is because when you encounter what looks like a difficulty, e.g. an inlet from the sea or something else you need to work around, you can simply insert extra waypoints that take you around the problem.

There is a drawback to this: the more waypoints you insert, the more time you'll spend staring at your GPS device, and miss that golden eagle that just flew by. So, use them only where necessary. If the route is dead straight, one waypoint at the start and one at the end is sufficient. Where *OS Maps* particularly helps here is the possibility it gives of switching from a conventional 'map' view to an 'aerial' view, akin to Google Earth. You can then zoom in on this aerial view and actually see trodden footpaths on the ground. This allows you to adjust the route, and thereby make it more accurate.

Compare the two routes in Figure 59. The aerial view has allowed adjustment of the waypoints a little to give a more accurate route description.

If you check the OS map closely, you can see several places where the route deviates from footpaths marked on the map. This has been achieved by using the aerial view to show me the actual footpaths. In this instance – it's a walk in a beautiful corner of Orkney – it doesn't make a significant amount of difference. But there will be many times when this benefit of *OS Maps* will come into its own.

Once you are satisfied with your route and its many waypoints, you need only to 'Save' it, and then 'Export' it as a GPX file that can then be copied into your GPS device for later use.

Fig. 59: The same route delineated on OS mapping and OS Maps aerial view

GPS essentials

A GPS can add immeasurably to your walking safety and enjoyment but keep in mind the points recapped below, and always take appropriate paper mapping of your route or the area in which you are walking.

Summary

1. *If you are a GPS first-timer, or using a new device, familiarise yourself with it in your local neighbourhood before walking with it in wild or remote countryside.*

2. *Allow your GPS to complete its start-up routine after switching it on.*

3. *Before beginning a walk, clear your GPS track memory and reset its trip computer. Remember at the end of your walk to save your track log, especially if you want to review the route in OS Maps.*

4. *Remember you need to be moving to activate your GPS compass pointer.*

5. *When walking with GPS and paper maps take regular notice of your device's positional readings and use these to check your progress on the map.*

6. *Check you have good satellite reception when making important navigation decisions.*

7. *Beware that tree cover, cliffs and overhanging rock may impair or interrupt signal reception.*

8. *Automatically recording point locations as you walk, your GPS builds a track log of your route and this can be used to retrace your steps.*

9. *In GPS terms, a route is a plan of where you want to go; a track is a record of where you have been.*

10. *Always carry spare batteries for your device or, for using an app on your mobile, ensure that your phone is fully charged before setting out.*

Index